Weavings 2000

POETRY FOR
THE NEW MILLENNIUM

EDITED BY MICHAEL S. GLASER

International Standard Book Number: 0-938572-28-8
Library of Congress Control Number: 00-134948

First edition printed 2000
Printed in the U.S.A.

Typography and cover design by Cynthia Comitz, *In Support, Inc.*
Cover photography by Richard Smolko, *Potomac Photography*
Printing by George Klear, *Printing Press, Inc.*

This book was made possible by a generous grant from the
Maryland Commission for Celebration 2000

Published by Forest Woods Media Productions, Inc.
for the
Maryland Commission for Celebration 2000

For information contact the editor:
Michael S. Glaser
Weavings 2000
St. Mary's College of Maryland
St. Mary's City, MD 20686

www.maryland2000.org

Introduction

Each of us has memories of how the written word has woven itself into and around our lives. I remember Gilbert Byron, travelling as a Maryland Poet-in-the-Schools, telling children the story of how Marianne Moore kept re-writing her long poem "Poetry" (the one that begins "I too dislike it") until it was reduced to a very few lines that end, "Reading it, however...one discovers...in it...a place for the genuine."

I often think it is exactly that "genuine" response to human experience which makes literature so important. As Robert Coles suggests, good writing, like a good friend, serves to challenge as well as comfort us, it "offers us other eyes with which we might see and other ears with which we might make soundings." Literature provides windows inward and windows through which we might look at worlds that are different from our own. And often, literature enables us to see how the people who inhabit those worlds are more similar to us than we first imagined. Stories and poems provide us places to explore both our human connections as well as our distinct human otherness.

Many believe that it is the writer's work to live genuinely, to embrace life fully and openly, and then to write about what is experienced and/or discovered. I think that the many voices in this anthology illustrate how that might be done. Such an examination of our lives is, of course, not always comfortable because in looking at who we are, we do not always see what we would wish or hope for. But almost always, the honesty and integrity of such examination enables us to better understand ourselves and others. W. H. Auden may well have been right when he suggested that it is only because we can recognize the sound of the authentic voice that we are able to prevent others from reducing the human experience to so many political sound bites, catchy advertisers' slogans or sweet greeting card sentimentalities.

I hope you will find within the pages here, something of what I have found: a stirring of response to genuine poems, food for the soul and spirit, challenges for the mind and heart, encouragement to be more awake, more thoughtful, and more alive.

Many people deserve appreciation for their help with this anthology. The editor would like to make special note of the following: Governor Parris Glendening who established the Maryland Commission for Celebration 2000; the chair of the Maryland Commission for Celebration 2000, the Honorable William Donald Schaefer; and the commission's vice chair, Dr. Jane Margaret O'Brien, president of St. Mary's College of Maryland. Also, Dr. Laraine Glidden, special assistant to the president at St. Mary's College, and chair of the education committee of the Maryland Commission for Celebration 2000. I also want to thank the entire staff of the commission whose work has nurtured and supported this project – especially Louise Hayman, executive director, and Alicia Moran, assistant director. Also to the members of the Maryland 2000 education committee who enthusiastically supported this anthology, and to the generous contributors to the Maryland Commission for Celebration 2000 who have underwritten this project, our appreciation and gratitude.

Additionally, recognition is due to a number of people whose hands-on efforts have literally given shape to this anthology: To Grace Cavalieri, always a guiding light for writers as well as for this anthology; to Kathryn Lange, associate editor, whose sensibilities inform this entire work; and to Eva Glaser, the assistant editor; to the editorial staff and our executive assistant, Serena Graham, whose clear-sightedness, organization and hard work have enabled this anthology to emerge out of an exciting morass of manuscripts and good intentions; to Pamela Dunne and the Maryland State Arts Council; to Colie Ring, Gail Wood, and Janet Haugaard; to Allyson McGill, Peggy Marshall, and Cindy Comitz; to Wayne Karlin and Lucille Clifton, and to the many writers whose contributions to the 21st Literary Festival at St. Mary's in the summer of 1999 have been abstracted and edited to serve as the thoughtful "weavings" that I trust will encourage you to pause and reflect in the process of reading through this anthology. And, finally, to the wonderful staff at St. Mary's College of Maryland who, for 21 years, have worked tirelessly in support of the Literary Festival from which this anthology blossomed and in which its roots are centered.

There are many, many lives, seen and unseen, named and unnamed, which have directly contributed to this anthology, to the poems and stories herein, to the poets and writers whose work is recorded within. The song of one voice is connected to others in a hundred thousand ways. Even as we advance into the future, we carry with us the astonishingly complex composition of our past. It is, perhaps, this very complexity of weavings that enables a good poem or story, memoir or essay to profoundly touch our lives.

I like to think of this anthology as a gift to you, the reader, from the Maryland Commission for Celebration 2000 in recognition of the millennium. It is a proud affirmation of the art and spirit which exist in and are nurtured by the land, the water and the people who comprise our fair state.

Enjoy!

Michael S. Glaser
St. Mary's City
April, 2000

Contents

At the end of our bloody century, we might well pray that our country will turn more and more to the life of the spirit, and, when it does, a national archive of the spirit will be found in our poetry.

.....Roland Flint

Poet Laureate of Maryland
at the turn of the millennium

A Major Work

Poems are hard to read
Pictures are hard to see
Music is hard to hear
And people are hard to love

But whether from brute need
Or divine energy
At last mind eye and ear
And the great sloth heart will move.

.....William Meredith

The Owl

Dusk in suburbia lies like a pall
over the gabled roofs. We drive quickly
down Charles Street, heading home toward the city
when all at once what looks like a knitted shawl –
something grandma might wear, mouldy with fringe –
comes sailing straight for our car window,
until it's blown off course. We feel a twinge,
and before it roosts in the hemlock, know,
though we've never seen one live, that it's an owl,
too timid we've been told for our society.
He blinks, readjusts his monastic cowl,
gives what I can only call a lustful squeal,
then pushes back against the mournful tree,
seizing the mouse struck dumb beneath our wheel.

....David Bergman

Still Life

I must explain why it is that at night, in my own house,
Even when no one's asleep, I feel I must whisper.
Thoreau and Wordsworth would call it an act of devotion,
I think; others would call it fright; it is probably
Something of both. In my living-room there are matters I'd
   rather not meddle with
Late at night.

I prefer to sit very still on the couch, watching
All the inanimate things of my daytime life –
The furniture and the curtains, the pictures and books –
Come alive,
Not as in some childish fantasy, the chairs dancing
And Disney prancing backstage, but with dignity,
The big old rocker presiding over a silent
And solemn assembly of all my craftsmen,
From Picasso and other dignities gracing my walls
To the local carpenter benched at my slippered feet.

I find these proceedings
Remarkable for their clarity and intelligence, and I wish I
   might somehow
Bring into daylight the eloquence, say, of a doorknob.
But always the gathering breaks up; everyone there
Shrinks from the tossing turbulence
Of living,
A cough, a creaking stair.

....Reed Whittemore

Thanksgiving Night: St. Michael's

Chesapeake Bay

A scarred night, fog, the sky a streaky white,
as we walk out, out on a finger of land
that points like a sign to World's End,
and step from land to water, the pier creaking
under us like the springs of an old bed.
We scare, by being here, a heron
from its hiding place; it changes itself
into blue smoke and wind and flies west
over the world's bright edge, leaving behind
an old ghost under the pier, the stiff ribs
of a skiff buried in black water. Eaten
by air, by water, each year there is less to it.
Behind us, a world too-human waits,
a crisscross of familiar streets and houses
painted with fresh paint, and lit storefronts,
their goods arranged in careful tiers and rows,
offering us the new, the young, the bright.
Skeletal night! Soon the tide will run out,
stranding the skiff, like a great beached fish,
in shallows, each bony rib countable, monstrous,
a feast of past, present, and future holidays
mingling, like wine in water, until all are one,
the dead, living, and not-yet-born gathered
around the great table to suck the sweet
marrow from the kill, as if there will always
be, for us, a tomorrow tomorrow.

.....Elizabeth Spires

Looking for Divine Transportation

I have wandered
into the Garden lured
by the fragrance and color

of delicate blossoms. Among
jabbering children speaking
innocent words I cannot repeat

and tragic characters in felt
hats, I search for those angels
who are wheels. With no visa

to be here, no encyclopedia
to guide me, I conjure
an image of you, let you

be my bible of common
sense: how to find my way
in; how to find the way out.

.....Karren Alenier

Poem of the Mother

The heart goes out ahead
scouting for him
while I stay at home
keeping the fire,
holding the house down
around myself
like a skirt from the high wind.

The boy does not know
how my eye strains to make out
his small animal shape
swimming hard across the future
nor that I have strengthened myself
like the wood side of this house
for his benefit.

I stay still
so he can rail against me.
I stay at the fixed center of things
like a jar on its shelf
or the clock on the mantel
so when his time comes
he can leave me.

....Myra Sklarew

Lotus Pond

Like uncoiling cobras summoned by flute,
stems rise, roused out of muck
by music, by the chance,

here again, to ripen and swell
until each leaf unfolds,
purple side down, pins

its green heart open
on a mirror
with ten thousand others

on a sheen of water-silk.
This is how compassion grows:
out of the mud,

mottled by bruise.
And this is what it asks:
among ten thousand stems

intertwined and swaying
in underwater twilight,
who can trace which stalk

to which flower?
Who can say which heart is mine?
Which yours?

....Barbara Hurd

Montana Terrace
(progression to natural)

In my neighborhood
mothers were mountains
their jagged hearts climbed by children
& husbands seeking elevation

men, weak with selfish intentions
chipped away at their souls
blasting caps of hatred
shook their foundations

bearing the load of family
they carried a race on their backs
a steep ascent to destiny

In my neighborhood
mothers were mountains
i have seen them crumble

& become women.

& love them still.

                    ....*Kenneth Carroll*

The Miracle of Bubbles

A woman drives to the video store
to rent a movie. It is Saturday night,
she is thinking of nothing in particular,
perhaps of how later she will pop popcorn
or hold hands with her husband and pretend
they are still in high school. On the way home
a plane drops from the sky, the wing shearing
the roof of her car, killing her instantly.
Here is a death, it could happen to any of us.
Her husband will struggle the rest of his days
to give shape to an event that does not mean
to be understood. Since memory cannot operate
without plot, he chooses the romantic – how young
she was, her lovely waist, or the ironic – if only
she had lost her keys, stopped for pizza.

At the precise moment the plane spiraled
out of control, he was lathering shampoo
into his daughter's hair, blonde and fine
as cornsilk, in love with his life, his
daughter, the earth (for "cornsilk" is how
he thought of her hair), in love with the miracle
of bubbles, how they rise in a slow dance,
swell and shimmer in the steamy air, then
dissolve as though they never were.

.....Barbara Goldberg

After Winter

He imagines his fingers
In the blacker loam
The lean months are done with,
The fat to come.

His eyes are set
On a brushwood-fire
But his heart is soaring
Higher and higher.

Though he stands ragged
An old scarecrow,
This is the way
His swift thoughts go

"Butter beans fo' Clara
Sugar corn fo' Grace
An' fo' de little feller
Runnin' space."

"Radishes and lettuce
Eggplants and beets
Turnips fo' de winter
An' candied sweets."

"Homespun tobacco
Apples in de bin
Fo' smokin' an' fo' cider
When de folks draps in."

He thinks with the winter
His troubles are gone;
Ten acres unplanted
To raise dreams on.

The lean months are done with,
The fat to come.
His hopes, winter wanderers,
Hasten home.

"Butter beans fo' Clara
Sugar corn fo' Grace
An' fo' de little feller
Runnin' space...."

....Sterling A. Brown

What stories are supposed to do is open doors. They allow directions for people to go.

....Wayne Karlin

Both writing and reading literature well often requires a descent into places we don't want to go. But when we genuinely explore our stories, we are able to come to the universal and thus we begin to understand the bridges that connect us.

....Maria Mazziotti Gillan

Taken From the Top

Mountaintop, we scan the valley
      as God must, entrusting
      life to all directions;
      the dollhouse family
      in matchstick dwelling,
Horse and cow minute,
      cropping grass cocoon
      mid toy dog's scamper
      on the Earth balloon.
How miniscule is man,
      how fragile his frame –
      without his soul,
He and the ant selfsame.

          ....Marijane G. Ricketts

First Days in a World

for Caroline

> Like hearing parents, some deaf parents also
> expect to have a child who is the same as
> themselves...[But in the case of deaf parents
> of hearing children,] how is it possible that
> parent and child from two such different
> worlds can meet?
> -Paul Preston, *Mother Father Deaf*

Right now, of everything that's visible
And yet means nothing, this shy man, your father
Deaf since birth, who's watched you for an hour,
May be most important. He's been told
His twin daughters, weeks premature, can hear,
But can't believe it yet, not till he sees
Some sign in your response beyond the glass
Dividing him from you. He taps the window,
Sensing its vibration; taps again,
And all the babies twitch. How small your hands
Are, flexing while your sister cries; and now
He knows – elated, saddened – *Time to go*,
The nurse touches his arm, and so he does,
Though when he finds your mother still asleep,
He'll have nowhere to go except the lobby
Or outside, to smoke...For you, whose newborn
Hands, short-fingered, dense with lines, close now
And fall down at your side, the world is what
Rocks you within its hum, all cries except
Your own drowned out, a bright machinery
That warms you in its shell. You want so much
Just to be held these first days in a world
More like his than you'll ever know again.

....*Ned Balbo*

Take Hold

If there is nothing
before you, take hold
of it. You may be fortunate
or not. Place it deep
in your pocket regardless.
It is a possession
as no other.

When you are to leave and
have made all your
preparations; when you
are ordered to declare all
your possessions, reach in
to the dark pocket.

This is a symbol
traveler, a parable
perhaps. Nothing
is as whole as the space
in the air
you pass through.
And it is yours. If
you will take hold of it.

....Merrill Leffler

Bee

For once I was not bent
on denying the worst scenario
but listened to the bee
get louder as it came closer.
I was still as the rumble moved
into my chest and the machinery
of its wings passed over.

*

The bee kept changing direction, mid-air
and the sound diminished or drew close randomly.
I've seen the brightest yellow flicker
do the same in a wet, green field
– take one sip, reverse itself
and look for some fresh thing because
it so loved the idea of abundance.

*

But I was only part of the abundance.
And who else would I be
so adorned, but clearly
an attractive thing to it,
a singular sweetness.
I mean, I was willing
to think like an ornament.

Then I saw myself as I was –
not nearly what it wanted.
I did not grow, like the rose,
dangerous and inviting
steps to my heart and my heart
was not perfect – hidden,
dusty and small.

*

In place of what it wanted,
I would do. And I saw
my two wild arms
in the air, waving,
not knowing how to say
I was more than that,
in its language.

.....Lia Purpura

Song of Herself

She sings a song
from the other room
and the notes and melody and the river of it
stream in to where I am,

where this person who was I is,
an I changed.

She's an orange, she's a sky,
a blue ball on the beach,
an annunciation.

She's this new song –
the notes fall and rise, warm and ticklish.

It was the sound of her, first,
like a *New Yorker* cartoon I saw once:
a *waah* from a bassinet, as if
the bassinet were alive, speaking, God's voice,
the joy the joy the joy
of sudden sound. (In the cartoon
it's funny. It is. It is funny.)

Her voice. Her small throat extends up
and her small mouth turns into an O and then –

her arms pull up and she pushes her hands
below her chin
and with her black eyes –
more distinct all the time, as if she is
pulling up from the soul of the world
to her own individual soul, and she's

so assuredly her own by now – she holds me,

she brings me. She brings me, the new me,
to the music hall. It is. It is!

.....*Aurelie Sheehan*

we are running

running and
time is clocking us
from the edge like an only
daughter.
our mothers stream before us,
cradling their breasts in their
hands.
oh pray that what we want
is worth this running,
pray that what we're running
toward
is what we want.

.....*Lucille Clifton*

Harriet Tubman Said...

There are many kinds of being scared:
hiding out with snakes in a swamp,
praying in a whisper so low the Lord
strains to hear. And in morning light
all gold and flashy, you trample down
marshweed beside the road, shivering at
every bird call, or you hold on
to some long, way back love, wishing
against all odds your name will come up
on his lips. Sometimes it's a brief glimpse
of old square-toed death, reared-up
on his hind legs, waiting.

My train only moves one way and it's up
a mountain. You left fear standing
in a field with a whip. He was your
running start. Now he's sniffing around,
licking your heels, tasting your sweat.
You turn and I see him behind your eyes.
He suits you fine 'cause he's all you had
for so long. But I'll tell you this,
you can't go back. Fear will never be
so close to you as this cold iron finger
I hold in your ear. You can only die once.
You can die now, or you can be free.

....Maxine Clair

Don't Undersell Yourself

Consider the brown cow
Eating green grass
Giving white milk

            ....Grace Cavalieri

This Is

The September of our loss

The old man who is to die
Takes a nap anyway

I admire that

            ....Grace Cavalieri

The Cheer

reader my friend, is in the words here, somewhere.
Frankly, I'd like to make you smile.
Words addressing evil won't turn evil back
but they can give heart.
The cheer is hidden in right words.

A great deal isn't right, as they say,
as they are lately at some pains to tell us.
Words have to speak about that.
They would be the less words
for saying *smile* when they should say *do*.
If you ask them *do what?*
they turn serious quick enough, but never unlovely.
And they will tell you what to do,
if you listen, if you want that.

Certainly good cheer has never been what's wrong,
though solemn people mistrust it.
Against evil, between evils, lovely words are right.
How absurd it would be to spin these noises out,
so serious that we call them poems,
if they couldn't make a person smile.
Cheer or courage is what they were all born in.
It's what they're trying to tell us, miming like that.
It's native to the words,
and what they want us always to know,
even when it seems quite impossible to do.

....*William Meredith*

If we don't tell our stories, we are in danger of allowing others to make up our stories for us. The writer has to be willing to risk going to that place where all loss and anger and love and sorrow and joy hide. We have to give ourselves permission to speak and write the truth.

....Maria Mazziotti Gillan

A serious shift from the need for endless acquisition that marks the "consumer culture" of the industrialized world at the end of the 20th century, toward praise and thanks, could help open our minds and hearts to respond with care to the pain – of people and of the planet – that also marks this millennial time on the planet. In a culture of praise, we might begin to truly face the injustice deeply present on our planet and move to heal it. A culture marked by praise, with heart and mind open to healing pain – this is a culture that I dream of helping to make. This is a culture that poets and writers have the power to help us all make.

....Sara Ebenreck

Charity

The sun rises for the dogs who are blinded
by light. One day strides with its long legs
into the next. Charity works in the passing.

And the woman is grateful for her heart which
lets her down, thankful for foxglove blooming,
taller than her hopes, in the spotted light beyond

the wall. A brown toad pulses, a worm makes
good dirt – a woman takes her heart for a walk.
All light will rise like heat; shadow will save her

– even a poppy guards its purple cunning. Such
heart beats there – good darkness, footsteps and
blunders, a blind dog finding its long, late way.

.....*Renée Ashley*

Poetry Sends Her Love

Suddenly I'm helping
to pack Poetry's car.
And good riddance I'm saying,
*What have you ever
done for me?* Poetry
is driving away, waving
farewell, leaving me
to my life.
A few months go by.

I open the refrigerator
door to find
some peaches: yellow and red,
each gathered square
and greenly toward its stem.
Against my fingers, a seam
runs down the center:
plush skin. I'm holding
one of the peaches
and standing there.

A few days later,
I get the letter. She hasn't
forgotten. Still eloquent,
everything spelled correctly,
a light perfume on fine bond in her
inimitable calligraphy:
Beloved, it says,
*everything has its beauty, you
as well, its form
inside that rises
to the skin. Did you get
those peaches?*

....Sam Schmidt

Driving on the Beltway

On the Beltway
I miss the earthliness.
Instead of the buoyant
steadiness

of forsythia's yellow, expectancy
of apple tree buds breathing
their white insides open
in fragrance, the coolness

of tulip leaves slowly unwrapping
in wisps of laughter,

I feel the push

of passing cars, the uneven
pavement, borders
of broken lines,
concrete barriers. While I count

the exits, the minutes crawl
along my spine, deposit lead
in my thighs. I long
for a whiff of chocolate mulch

freshly piled around the trees.
To stop.
To touch the porous skin.
To be touched.

....Danuta E. Kosk-Kosicka

Our Mother Serves Glamour for Breakfast

"Glamour isn't everything."
Judy Garland declares from the TV screen.
Our mother says, "Don't believe her,"
Our mother could have been in show business
if she hadn't gotten stage fright so bad
each spring at dance recital.
She sings and shuffles off to Buffalo
in her fluffy pink slippers,
red toenails poking out.
My sister and I chew our Wheaties,
wonder who will get the prize in the box.

Our mother scours the kitchen sink,
buffs the metal cabinets
til their chrome shines
like the kitchen floor.
She sings, "Oh What a Beautiful Morning"
and all the songs from Oklahoma
as she mops dust out the door
of our project apartment.

I clear away the breakfast bowls
as she sits my sister on the table for therapy.
Her strong hands mold
my sister's crooked feet,
bend my sister's limp legs
back and forth
back and forth trying to wake the muscles.

My sister is four.
She wants to be a ballerina.
Our mother says yes.
She will sew a tutu with the colors of the rainbow.
She sings to her,

"You must have been a beautiful baby,
cause Baby, look at you now"
I tap-dance my Ginny dolls across the linoleum.

There was another man my mother
might have married,
She might have got a job in Europe
if my father's eyes had not been so blue.
Before she met our father,
she got her picture on the front page
outside the theater, the day she skipped school
to see Frank Sinatra.

Now she's off to clean the bathroom.
On her knees she scrubs the tub and toilet,
the white powder turns to blue.
"Put your dreams away for another day,
darling...." Her voice echoes against pink ceramic.
My sister and I hum along.
We agree.
Glamour is everything.

.....Laura K. Lynds

Maundy Thursday

You don't want to hear this old story, green as it is. Yes,
the early sun. Girls in pinafores snap sticks on the cobbled
street, their hair even shines – this light after a storm
stuns something in all of us. Water rushes the mill trench,
long heavy ribbons. Geese sleep tucked in shade. And the corn
rail stands so high. Why do we want what we have as we leave it?
Why then go at all? Looking South now, from this hill, nothing
but sea after sea, a possible circumnavigation of swollen water
in one state or another from here to here again. And what?
The newly turned earth beside you is not enough? The pair
of white butterflies reminding you *go barefoot*? Didn't Spring
always find you perched in some high sunned place? Like this?

....*Robin Holland*

Waking

for Mackenzie, age 2

She wakes in her new bed, calling out my name.
As my head rises from the pillow, she smiles.
She asks me if she can wake up now,
as if to make sure it is morning
and not dark anymore.

She climbs out of her bed and into mine,
places her yellow knitted blanket on my lap
and rests her head on my knee.

I gaze at her, trying to imagine
what is going through her mind.
I think she is a wonder.

She asks for a drink of water
and we go to the kitchen
where I pour her a cup.

She carefully climbs onto her chair
at the table, and drinks
while I stare at her in amazement
watching how carefully
she sips and puts the cup down –
every movement distinct, important.
Then softly, she reaches her hand to mine.

On this cold morning, I am filled
with warmth. I smile,
learning more every day
what is truly important.

....Eva Glaser

Lies

Lies are the worst thing I know.
Lies are like a bouncing ball
that goes on and on.

Before you know it
the ball will stop
and just be waiting there
like an endless pit
or a mom's disappointed stare.

.... Tyler Anderson

Marquee

When does the applause for fall's splendor
Become the grey silence of winter?
I try each year, but can never catch the last act.

Each time I am sure I can see the warm yellow stage,
The final red curtain,
The last leaf fall
Before the lights go down and the cold comes.

But they finish while I am on the road,
Moving through a colorful blur,
Driving too fast to get home.

Where is fall's schedule posted?
How can I be on time?
If the signs were left up,
At least I could read what I missed,

But as soon as the season is over
They are taken down, thrown away. Then
Winter posts its own coming attractions
And advance tickets for spring.

.....Kate Richardson

Chartres Cathedral

You will see Chartres Cathedral, they said, eight
or nine miles from the town. And so we did,
Windshield wipers sweeping at
the flashing rain. Wheat stacked each side

of the road. Out of mist, two spires rose.
Peguy had walked this way: one pilgrim more
in centuries of pilgrims. We tried to teach our eyes
to hold the ancient church. But the town was there

and we in the narrow street before the Royal Door.
Blue windows of Chartres, and God creating man
in joyful stone; gargoyle and buttress – clear
in sunlight after rain. What we had known

we realized: glass is flame, stone
is story; love is reaped where love was sown.

....Sr. Maura Eichner

The Mystery of the Caves

I don't remember the name of the story,
but the hero, a boy, was lost,
wandering a labyrinth of caverns
filling stratum by stratum with water.

I was wondering what might happen:
would he float upward toward light?
Or would he somersault forever
in an underground black river?

I couldn't stop reading the book
because I had to know the answer,
because my mother was leaving again –
the lid of the trunk thrown open,

blouses torn from their hangers,
the crazy shouting among rooms.
The boy found it impossible to see
which passage led to safety.

One yellow finger of flame
wavered on his last match.
There was a blur of perfume –
mother breaking miniature bottles,

then my father gripping her,
but too tightly, by both arms.
The boy wasn't able to breathe.
I think he wanted me to help,

but I was small, and it was late.
And my mother was sobbing now,
no longer cursing her life,
repeating my father's name

among bright islands of skirts
circling the rim of the bed.
I can't recall the whole story,
what happened at the end....

Sometimes I worry that the boy
is still searching below the earth
for a thin pencil of light,
that I can almost hear him

through great volumes of water,
through centuries of stone,
crying my name among blind fish,
wanting so much to come home.

....Michael Waters

Good writing invites us, as writers and readers, to immerse ourselves in a very particular landscape, an immersion which helps us open to new and richer ways of seeing ourselves and our surroundings. I think of these immersions as opportunities 1) to move from the abstraction to the particular; 2) to reconsider our notion of beauty; 3) to read and write without cynical detachment or heart-bleeding sentimentality, but in full acknowledgement of the cycles of birth and death and rebirth; 4) to associate, at least once in a while, with histories that are not "made in our image"; 5) to realize that our spiritual and imaginative selves might be at least partly shaped by something other than we thought.

....Barbara Hurd

We can't heal the world until we can heal ourselves.

....Grace Cavalieri

Minnow

I see myself as a minnow,
Small to the rest of the world.
I don't know what's happening,
Or what's going to happen –
But I swim with the waves,
The constant beating sound of drums.

As the sun rises,
And the waves glimmer,
I begin each day with courage,
Wandering in the depths of the ocean.
Not an agenda to follow,
Just swimming and swimming and swim-
ming.

....Tracey Slaughter

A Fortunate Catch

The gill looks like a wound,
doesn't it? Hooked by the scythe
of a crescent moon that held him
dangling, he dropped here, raw.

A mouth looks like that
in a candid shot, caught
at a barbecue, as the jaws
fall open in surprise.

Twisting and trying to swim
in sand now, the bluefish
for all the show is helpless.
Here, at shore's edge,

the sea washes up foam,
10 a.m., paying back the moon
her low interest loan.
The fish's old sunken eye

never closes. Shaped like a tear,
the fish is trying to pull
away from itself. Again the tail
lifts into the air, reaches

for small planets, lost home seas.
Now it raises its thin red veils,
begins to move seaward. Take note,
you flies and dragonflies,

you sandpipers and starfish.
Here comes a little life!
Sing out, call for it. Did I mention
how the fin resembles a wing?

....*Jacklyn W. Potter*

Still Life
in chalk on asphalt

Muggy August is in the house,
the thick air sticking a shirt
into the curve of your back.
You go out for a banana Slurpee,
close the door like the cover of a book,
tilt your head and hope for rain.
The stars stand out like grains of salt
spilled across a black tablecloth.
You hang a right on the Ave,
pass the Liquor store's grinning Colt .45 sign.
The moon shines like a cue ball about to break up
the hustlers clustered on the corner.
Jeans hang loose on their hips,
their noses sniff for the smell of green.
You shake your head to the question
yellowing in their eyes.
A Jeep booms by, trailing a ribbon of rapping,
its tires whispering circular secrets
into the asphalt's ear.
Around the corner where the 7-11 sits,
the rotating arm atop an ambulance
slaps two paramedics crouched
over a young boy in the street.
His eyes and mouth are drawn open,

the thought balloon above him, empty.
Cherry Kool-Aid stains his shirt,
his sneakers are white as a kilo of coke.
All the trees have their arms in the air.
The witness' fingers disagree
on the number of shots.
His mother collapses against a mailbox,
weary lines penciled on her face,
dark blues bleeding down the back of her throat.
Her cheeks shiny under watercolored eyes,
fingers soaked with a fleeting soul,
she cradles his cooling body,
his name sits crooked on her lips.
The parked cars stare silently ahead
as the sound of red begins to reign.

....dj renegade

Trying Out a Blazer 4-By

A hundred and sixty five horses over
a truck chassis – it rides high and the view
opens beyond car-lot fence to fields,
to hills. On the road I'm level with an Exxon tanker,
as we pass the driver lifts a thumb in greeting.

I am unused to the quick response, the surge
uphill, I've settled for what's adequate,
but the sly taste of power meagers that, an appetite
wakes for steeper slopes, rougher tracks.

A bicyclist yaws against the grade, his dog
loping beside him, I gun the motor and they're
a blip in the rearview mirror. Enhanced
by a V-8 engine and the arrogance it bestows,
a hidden penchant to belittle outs, with a rush
of scorn I pull past a white sedan,
the woman driving, gray-haired as I.

Wait, hold on. This is how wars begin.

I downshift and swerve onto a lumber road,
shocks take the washboard bumps, wheels
crush a burst of Christmas fern but a fallen
pine tree blocks my way. I stop, kill
the motor and sudden silence clamps in.

Then rustle, tick, the sharp slice of a jay's
call and a drift of something heady, sweet
I cannot name. Just as well this halt
to turbulence that skewed me from a well-mapped
path. It's not the loosing of horses I fear,
but the unbridled wilderness opened in my belly.

...Ann B. Knox

Don't Postpone Joy

a butterfly
minus
cell phone,
contacts,
or resume,

skitters
along the
somber buildings
of farragut square.

does not crowd
into the ubiquitous
buffet by the
pound
delicatessens
that will close

like broken wings
at rush hour,

choosing instead
to be guided by /

to dine on the wind

we promise ourselves
we too will kiss

when we retire

....reuben jackson

Christmas Eve: My Mother Dressing

My mother was not impressed with her beauty;
once a year she put it on like a costume,
plaited her black hair, slick as cornsilk, down past her hips,
in one rope-thick braid, turned it, carefully, hand over hand,
and fixed it at the nape of her neck, stiff and elegant as a crown,
with tortoise pins, like huge insects,
some belonging to her dead mother,
some to my living grandmother.
Sitting on the stool at the mirror,
she applied a peachy foundation that seemed to hold her down,
    to trap her,
as if we never would have noticed what flew among us unless
    it was weighted and bound in its mask.
Vaseline shined her eyebrows,
mascara blackened her lashes until they swept down like feathers;
her eyes deepened until they shone from far away.

Now I remember her hands, her poor hands, which, even then
    were old from scrubbing,
whiter on the inside than they should have been,
and hard, the first joints of her fingers, little fattened pads,
the nails filed to sharp points like old-fashioned ink pens,
    painted a jolly color.
Her hands stood next to her face and wanted to be put away,
    prayed

for the scrub bucket and brush to make them useful.
And, as I write, I forget the years I watched her
pull hairs like a witch from her chin, magnify
every blotch – as if acid were thrown from the inside.

But once a year my mother
rose in her white silk slip,
not the slave of the house, the woman,
took the ironed dress from the hanger –
allowing me to stand on the bed, so that
my face looked directly into her face,
and hold the garment away from her
as she pulled it down.

.... Toi Derricotte

Fires at Yellowstone

My mother calls today
with news of the Pennsylvania sun
burnt the color of candied oranges,

of noon turned dusk by faraway
disaster. How can it be?
Then Jack reminds me

of Mount St. Helens' ash
that darkened the sky it fell
through, of rice fields smoldering

in the California of his youth, the ash
settling on the hopscotch of Sacramento's
rooftops and lawns.
The current misplaced darkness

is from well-traveled smoke
that once was trees,
thousands and thousands of acres of trees
left to burn naturally too long.

When I was nine, I stood beside Old Faithful.
Snapshots confirm
that in my green Nehru jacket
I bounded from the '63 Ford wagon;

and in the dream beyond the photo,
the geyser reached up toward the Tetons or Sierras,
drifting mist across the wheat fields of Kansas,

across Indiana smokestacks and the long pull
of Ohio, before settling on a small town
in the Alleghenies, which was home.

The day my son was born
every tree in my body was razed,
and this great pain burnt thousands of acres
of everything I thought I could be.

It's October,
and our own paling Maryland sun leaves
a little earlier now;
my son asks where it goes.

And when I tell him how far
Earth must turn,
I think of Yellowstone,

I think of saplings sprouting from the body
that has been so blackened and enriched by disaster.

...Julia Wendell

For Chris

to you who said your father threw you
through the living room window who showed me
the scars from your neck to your navel
where the doctors cut open to fix
the eleven-year-old valves of your heart
there are things we hear with our calcareous hearts
that will drive us from the sanctified natures of our rooms
into the cold vast skies of a moonless night
where each star with its own blinking language
reveals unreachable solitude to us
I walked my angers till I ran out of streets
and barking dogs remembering the hours I spent
as a child listening to the sound of love
weeping through the walls of our house
from the welts of our father's embraces
the only ones he ever knew what can I tell you
but that love is an inparticular compass
that there is only one true angel
and her name is Innocence and the only choice
children have is to make laughter and play
out of melancholy I walked past the last street lamp
and stood in the shivering loneliness
of a dark road that led to some forever
I could no longer see though I was aware
of my blindness and of the impalpable sounds
of struggling gasps I have heard
coming from my own son when he is unable to catch
a single breath as he tries to muffle
the anguished and flailing love of his father
life is truly the most beautiful tragedy
I thought finding no wisdom or comfort in that
I turned back and as I turned I heard the lament
of a siren and the mongrels who quickly joined in

that harmony of sorrows piercing the darkness
erasing my footfalls and as I walked away I turned
to search that unplaceable howl and saw an explosion
of moonlight rising along the arc
of a perfect evening and I remembered what we see
and hear is only half of a story
you who stirred my silent dominions
who startled the fallen forms of purity introducing me
to all your fifth grade friends and who said
the thing you liked best is to go fishing
whenever your father comes to visit you thank you
thank you for guiding me back to my faith
in the powers of mystery

.... *Edgar Silex*

Bedtime Story

Something small and dark lay crouched
at the back of my throat
waiting its slow souring wait
until it would wait no longer.

The boy was already cowering;
the words he'd said had dropped
like a heavy, poisonous dram
swirling the waters of our anxious love.

Who can tell why this needed
to be said, or why the closed bolt
of my rage could not hold tight against it?

It was the same old thing,
me calling him out for the forming man
in him filling the child's mouth with words.

Don't talk back to your father, I said.

But the spell would not be cast this time.
That man possessed the quavering child
and only the pale child's shell
stood before me. A voice like my own
unleashed a black hail against the trigger
of my resolve.

And that dark thing
knew that its time had come again,
wheeled on fierce wings and grew
immense as the winter night.

I'd had to let go to gain myself back,
but the boy had no defense against it:
he could neither run nor strike it down,
only let it do its horror and spend itself
as all the demons finally do that spring from us,
unwanted, changing the colors of our hearts.

.....Phillip K. Jason

Returning to the City By Boat

A young girl stiffens her arm
in the shrill of a whistle.
Her cheeks harden and she points ashore
to a square light in a far building
echoing 'home, home'
as if she'd come home
from school this way for years,
shuffling these lights
like stones along the street.

And facing these lights, trembling
as the boat drifts
near, I watch this girl beside me
fingering the hem of her lace
dress, holding it to her knees,
keeping warm. And hear mother
in the next room stitching
clothes at night, waves
of cloth piling onto the floor,
darker as the hems grow deep.

And I remember as the bay
strays into harbor and twelve
herons watch the city dredge
stars from the night,
that we have no home but space
between two hems.

The girl lowers her thin arm,
wind falls into a pleat
of waves, my dress curls around
my white knees, as the young girl
clutches the iron railing and leans
over, far down, home into the streets.

.....Kathy Wagner

Depression

You start out with a tree in the ground
You get shade and fruit and color
And it's great

Then they take away the ground, leaving you the tree
And though the tree is dying
You still get shade and color
You remember the fruit
And it's okay

Then they take away the tree, leaving you
  a leaf
And though you've lost a lot
You still get the color
You remember the shade
But you forget about the fruit
And it's ...fine

Then they take away the leaf, leaving you a stem
And though it's not much by itself
You can remember the color
But you forget about the shade
And the fruit is long gone
And it's bad

Then they take away the stem, leaving you with
  nothing
And now there's nothing there
You've forgotten all the colors
The shade has long since passed
And you don't even know what fruit is, now
And the clinical name
Is depression

....Ben Moldover

At the Library

See the young girl
beside the window
bending over a book,
her dark hair shines
with floating dust fired
by sun tilting through glass.
See how she lifts her face
to the wall, seeing nothing,
seeing everything.
She is not here,
yet she is here.
I see her motionless,
tense but perfectly still.
She rides the invisible
flow of inspiration,
on a stream of language,
probes her own ideas
fused with vast musings
from the book she holds
open with slim fingers.
She fashions her own visions
guarded by a mysterious smile,
suspends the moment – a flash
where life gushes and flows
in a fountain of light.
My heart tells me
the young gather food
for the mind as naturally
as sparrows hunger for ripe
seeds sorted from grass.

....Stacy E. Tuthill

Passage of a Hunter

for Alden Capen

Now unseen, you stalk
invisible deer in the forest.
Wind gusts suddenly.
Crows lift ahead of you
in a clamor of fright as
dead leaves blow like
spume in your wake.

And I am frightened.
You are becoming something
random, unknown, the green
man melting into oak
wild as what you hunt.

.....*Kathy Pearce-Lewis*

Proof

Today the maples become
suddenly generous, showering
their webbed pods everywhere.
The screens go up. Front to back,
wind blows through the house.
Neighbors appear in their yards:
two women rasp at each other
over a fence, as if rediscovering
their voices. Dogs bark back
and forth in shade. The postman
comes by on foot, drops
a letter in my box.
                    Three days ago,
a friend was thinking of me.
What more proof do I need?
Out on the river, the last splinter
of ice returns to the river.

....Kathy Mangan

my diRtY SaVIoR

The burning bush doesn't mean much anymore.
The neighbor's children are playing with matches again.
The water from the rock we had to filter
In order to remove the dangerous bacteria.
So what if you believe that it's the body and the blood?
When everything is proven and nothing is believed
Our minds begin to wander
And we slowly turn to a different savior.
He writes our music and parades it as our own.
He reads us stories he has written to fill us with himself.
He paints us pictures in our minds and barters them for souls.
And we listen to the music, and we study all the stories,
And we see his pretty pictures, and we want to believe.
He becomes our work and our home,
He becomes our night and our day,
He becomes our life and our Death.
Corrupt, ancient, cunning, weak,
He is our dirty savior.
Why do we need an obsolete trinity
When a god with a billion faces can bring us sweetness and addiction?
As he slips deep inside our fragile skin
The spirit blesses us in silver
While Jesus bleeds green on the cross.

....Brian Wood

This Side of the Wall

Sometime they'll give a war and nobody will come.
– Carl Sandburg

Nineteen, and reflected alone in dark marble
the polished black wall stretches hungrily
and I tumble back thirteen years
to the very same place, where at six years old
I sat cross legged in the grass and watched
the sun dancing with the chetry leaves.

19 years before, a boy decided it would be easier
to put a bullet through his left foot
than face the jungle at night.

The night belonged to Charlie.

I was still learning my alphabet
and stared at the glorious tumble of letters
chiseled in dark marble
and scattered with roses.

Papa, you must have made a handsome soldier.

In a small wooden box in the corner of the basement,
a snapshot,
my father playing checkers on a pile of sandbags,
his helmet in his lap,
one hand on a rifle.

At six years old I watched his reflection stare back at him
until I couldn't tell which side of the black marble he belonged on.
with a gasp I took his hand
just to be sure.

His thumb ran deliberately over a line of letters
wiping away where tears should have been.
"He was my best friend,"
he whispered, eyes heavy and unmoving.

At six years old the wall of letters became words
and words became names
                    became fathers
                              holding hands with could-have been daughters
   who will never learn the alphabet
      or the sun in the cherry leaves.

At six years old through the thick smell of sun warmed flowers
a nightmare
rolled tightly in olive drab
and tucked away in my father's bottom drawer
unfolded freshly in me.

They left my father for dead with a hole in his chest
in mud so stagnant it rotted his toenails.

In the bedroom of a six-year-old girl
with cinnamon braids falling across a pillowcase printed with roses
the night again belonged to Charlie.

My father spent his 21st birthday pissing on himself
in a foxhole curled up like a baby
crying for his mother and
begging for his life
from any god he could dream of.

When I'm tipsy in a short skirt
dancing to Happy Birthday
with a beer in my hand and a friend on each arm
I will remember
and thank those same gods for my
enduring innocence.

.....Kathryn Lange

Bismillah

Let's break bread together.
Let's break challah.
When we break it let's say *bismillah*
which means *in God's name*.
For when the Lord has torn and
healed your heart
you will never be the same.
This bread is braided
the way we are all woven into one.
This bread is made with eggs.
To serve the Lord forever more
is all I'll ever beg of my mother.
She is none other than the same true God.
I thank her for my birth
and my work and my rest
and this bread.
I thank her for the sweet green earth
my feet are blessed to tread.

.....*Robert Francis Strott*

I grew up in three cultures simultaneously, but I learned to love and to take part in all three of those identities. When someone says I am half something, a half-breed, I say I am never half of anything. I am always a full Indian, a full Chicano, or a full American. Never part. My blood is not divisible.

....Edgar Silex

As we begin the new millennium, we are not just standing in the doorway, but before a mirror. Who do we want to be? Literature helps us engage meaningfully in the search for answers to that question, and the best of today's poets and writers help by reminding us of what it means to be human. They speak with truth, and that alone is redemptive.

....Elizabeth Lund

Rural Maryland

In rural Maryland I mistook a barn
for a church.
Painted white with long, vertical windows.
A spiritual place surrounded by tall grass.

The September brown field.

Nearby, the transcendent smoke
my blue emotion
rose from a small chimney.

.....Alan Britt

Freedom Ride

from the back of the bus
I can hear the wind outside
splashing against the hull

of seats as if this was the
shores of Africa during rush
hour and the slave trade is

steered by a driver who never
learned the words to Amazing
Grace

bless me Father for knowing
the difference between unemployment
and freedom

bless me Father for replacing
chains with change and tokens
and transfers

bless me Father for this window
which turns away the stares
and the eyes filled with despair

bless me Father
as I sit here in the back of
the bus wondering about the

absence of your power and presence

....E. Ethelbert Miller

The Thrower of Stones

"He threw a stone," Mother said,
decades after Grandfather was buried,
"across the fishpond and killed his brother."
He threw a stone, he was nine or ten,
playing in the family courtyard in Sin Wei,
our ancestral village in China. He had been told
to look after his little brother. He was
keeping him amused, slinging stones
in their ornamental pool
to fool the fish into rising for food.
The sun was shining, it was the morning
of his life, a morning like any morning,
with nothing to do except disturb
the equilibrium of carp and koi
by making ripples with the gravity of stones.
He was proud of his strength, impatient
with his brother's short tosses.

"Watch me!" he called across the circular
cement wall that held fish and water in place.
He pulled back his arm and sent his strength
into the stone, saw it arc through air, saw
the unspeakable, unstoppable landing,
the sudden released red
in his brother's forehead.
All at once the sunlight was too bright,
his ears lost the ability to hear.

His eyes could not blink.
Images burned into the darkness,
the exposed negatives behind his eyes:
his brother's puckering brow,
the slow toppling of the body over
the cement wall, into the dark water.

His hearing returned with the splash
and the shadows, large and small,
weaving and dancing about the pale form.
He saw his brother's hand wave
as if to say, "Follow me, the water's cool."
Reason later knew it had been just
the refraction of light and moving water.
Reason could explain, it could not
stop his vision, always the red hole
in that forehead, the silent (it is always
silent) falling and then, the splash of
displaced water, the pale hand moving
sluggishly as if tired, overcome by sleep.

Grandfather never knew the story of Cain
and Abel, but he left China, lived out his days
in an alien land. For what he had done,
even though accidentally, exile, instinct told him,
was the only bearable solution.

....Hilary Tham

Primer

Hands. eyes. mouth. nose. teeth
Smile. knees. ankles. feet,
Walk. At two, I learn
"my" alphabet. My
hands. My feet. My face.
My teeth, nose, eyes, on
and on. I recite words
out loud then find the shape –
matchings like socks. Each
sound, a mirror of outward
appearance, like pant legs, always two:
two eyes two hands two lips – one mouth
speaks and learns things are
as they exist. And my compact
vocabulary builds into dictionaries I must
abandon, forget in another season,
when births of the spirit teach my body
that things are not only as they exist:
            simile, symbol, metaphor, irony.

I know now that I am born
to lose my body only, not the shared
with you, dearest comrade –
smiles, evoked from Heart's hidden stirrings, moving
      like leaves on meditations' winds – and if lucky – I learn,
we are born, Contingent, born into a new
alphabet of knowledge, ancient and sacred:
      learn Gardens, whose blossoms
are not here only, but blooming
invocations to Invisible Becoming,
to the Unknowable. And so this
is all I am now, friend: Poetry, Spirit –
      And Prayer: My eyes, my hands,
mouth....
      Clothed by Love, I
walk back into Eden, unafraid,
with you.

....Donna Denizé

I hear a woman's voice
Without looking I know it is Mary Nelson.
I hear her voice,
        Bless us, O Lord, and these, our gifts

and I want to just sit and listen

because that's the blessing my family says
        that's the blessing my family has said
            every night we have eaten a meal together
            in restaurants, at campground picnic tables, at our table
        that's the blessing that each of us still say silently
            even when we are apart

apart

like Mary Nelson is, in the mental hospital.

eating her lunch in a room full of people
who have slit marks on their wrists,
who hear voices, who have bruises
under their eyes

She says this blessing
And she says the blessing out loud.

I don't turn to look at her
but I can see her smile
because maybe she's thinking,
like I am

of all the blessings said with our own families
holding hands around the table
feeling each others' skin
as we

give thanks

for these, our gifts.

.....*Anne McCauley*

Sunday Afternoon

for my brothers

Rolling into a patch of sunlight
laughing without reason
spreading the scent of summer grass
over our similar bodies
we are caught in agelessness.
Inside the dark house
our father is arguing.
He placed his joy of life
and eyes of discovery
into our making.
We golden haired children
are tumbling
from shadow to sunlight
in a stranger's yard
trying to share this gift
help him remember
the caressing itch
of grass meeting skin
and the yellow green
perfume of abandon.

.....Lara Payne

Posthumous

Would it surprise you to learn
that years beyond your longest winter
you still get letters from your bank, your old
philanthropies, cold flakes drifting
through the mail-slot with your name?
Though it's been a long time since your face
interrupted the light in my door-frame,
and the last tremblings of your voice
have drained from my telephone wire,
from the lists of the likely, your name
is not missing. It circles in the shadow-world
of the machines, a wind-blown ghost. For generosity
will be exalted, and good credit
outlasts death. Caribbean cruises, recipes,
low-interest loans. For you who asked
so much of life, who lived acutely
even in duress, the brimming world
awaits your signature. Cancer and heart disease
are still counting on you for a cure.
B'nai Brith numbers you among the blessed.
They miss you. They want you back.

....Jean Nordhaus

On Being a Witness at My Husband's Citizenship Hearing

Reliable as any wife,
I solemnly certify the moral fitness
of my husband. What is a citizen
if not loyal? I swear
he's always been able to support
himself, never broke a law on that long list,

that, as far as I know, he's not communist.
This judge suspects an alien inner life –
trouble spots not on the passport
to which I must have access.
I suppose I could mention the underwear
scissored from silken

antelope hide. How his yen
for certain customs in bed persists.
How unfamiliar his tint of hair
still is. How wild language survives
in his sleep like a goddess
so that his waking is, well, an effort –

all the dark evidence he didn't report.
But no. I'll continue to spy and listen
I confess
with the subversive joy of a pacifist.
I want my arms around other lives
that would, in a different dream, keep me scared.

The judge will compare
him to the solid home born sort,
will contrive
to remodel the nature I've chosen
to love. Though I'm no purist
I confess

I too have longed to possess
that stranger. When stuck in the solitaire
of my tribal dream, I tried to insist
on full disclosure, as though I could convert
the deepest language of another. I was mistaken.
We are ourselves, no matter how far we live
                    from home.

                    .....Karen Sagsetter

Vines

Though you would get tough
in August, uproot garlands
of honeysuckle and ivy,

the vines never gave ground.
They circle through privet,
forsythia, around each other

the way marriage wound
a thicket over us, rambling
at first, branching with children,

resting between seasons.
I unravel wild trumpets
from wisteria,

pull down creepers
tangled on lilacs,
but can no longer tell

within our maze
which strands were mine,
which ones began with you.

....*Elizabeth Follin-Jones*

The Ghosts In Our Bed

to my husband
who has Early Onset Parkinson's Disease

The mahogany four-poster bed your mother left us
is high up off the floor. It folds us into
the smell of lavender in sheets sprinkled with violets
the thick blue and green comforter.
For years we are happy in it,
lusty and young and so alive together,
this safe place to which we return each night
to lie in each other's arms, warm and exactly
where we want to be.

Now, when we climb into our bed, those people
who for so many years were ourselves, the ghosts
that we live with, sleep between us.

You have become so fragile. You are always
cold and need extra blankets, and you sleep
so quietly, your arms folded across your chest,
that when I wake up in the night, I have to reach out
to find you because I'm not certain you're there.

You used to take up so much space, with your energy
and strength, the big bones of your body.
I pile blankets on you, now,
your face rigid and frozen even in sleep.
The ghosts of the future hover over us, reminding us
every night of how much more we have to lose,
even as our old ghosts whisper, "Remember, remember."
I fall asleep with my hand on your shoulder,
to keep you with me as long as I can.

....*Maria Mazziotti Gillan*

Anytown

"I told you to get in the car, damn it!"

This is a town of many kids and little patience,
of many trees and little time to watch the trees
sway when a wind blows up from the south,
under April sun, causing the kids to jump
and dart through the stripmall parking lot.

This is a town of many roads and little signs,
of many ways to go and little time to hear the clouds
course, in effortless banter, across the April sky,
causing the kids to jump and dart through
the stripmall parking lot.

This is a town of many trucks and little Fords,
of many yellow lights run and little time to smell
cut grass, the wet walks behind, under the sprinkler
causing the kids to jump and dart through
the stripmall parking lot.

This is a town of many moods and little dogs,
of many clocks and little time to taste the wild berries
shining darkly on the median, under the birthday
playland sign, causing the kids to jump and dart
through the stripmall parking lot.

This is a town of many parents and little kids,
of many ways to love and little time for these kids,
under their South Park tee shirts.

.....Neal Dwyer

The Kind of Woman to Marry

November 13, 1998

Dear Josh and Eamon,

We didn't go to the islands or Paris on our honeymoon.
We went to Cape May, NJ, where the proprietor of a B&B refused
us shelter because we arrived at 3 a.m. after an all night drive.

That first night we slept on the beach by the nun's convent
near the lighthouse. It was freezing and my new bride (your mother)
and I clung to each other for warmth.

Since that night, many others have slammed doors in our
faces. Always, we've clung to each other near the outgoing tide
and laughed with each sunrise after the cold, harsh night.

> So marry a woman like that –
> one like your mother
> one who shelters you
> from the cold and dark
> both human and nature.

Love,

Dad

....Bruce Curley

Morning Quatrains

for Ynez

When daylight arrived, shrouded
In the pretext of morning
Fog, I had almost forgotten what it was
I wanted to say.

Then soft air landed
On the balcony
Of pink and fuchsia impatiens,
The ones that seduce hummingbirds

Like clockwork each noon
As the sun crawls onto wooden planks,
Serene under shadows
Of black metal railings

Where warmth dances against my skin
And I am kissing my wife
Who is miles away
Charting the delicate flow

Of misguided hands,
How automobiles clash
As if bumblebees tangling
Over a bright yellow sunflower.

I want to tell her I'm safe,
That I miss her
Here, amid words gently colliding
Among the countless seedlings

That have now grown like children.
When I water them, I say,
"She'll be home around six."
And they always listen,

Drinking what I whisper,
Thoughts of her
Sinking into their roots,
As I turn them, I hear them sing her name.

....*Jeffrey Lamar Coleman*

Lydia

There was life before us

my sister and I discovered,
looking at photographs

we shouldn't have been looking at
of the English girl my father

was engaged to during the war.
Here she is right in front of our eyes,

the woman before my mother,
in a black lace cocktail dress,

a cigarette in a holder,
pensive, earthy – waiting

in front of the carved wooden radio,
for news from the front.

This is the war, after all,
and here she is again, somewhere

on an English beach, draped
across my father's shoulder

all of her silky skin radiant
above the soft folds of sun dress.

They stand in front of a sign
that reads "Seaside Cottages,

two dollars." And here she is
again, painted onto the cockpit

of my father's plane with hardly
anything on at all, and here he is

in his flight jacket, looking
in fact, happy. My sister and I each

lift our pencils like cigarettes,
taking long sultry drags to puff

out invisible rings. They rise
in the air like silver nooses

that will catch our father
and hold him to us.

....Geraldine Connolly

One step in preparing for the next millennium is to remember that
while on some people's calendar — the Christian one — this may be a
turn of time loaded with symbolism, it's just another year in the
Islamic, Jewish, Buddhist, etc., calendars — And to the DNA in our
cells or the red-shift of the stars, it's just a millisecond ticking in the
long clock of time.

....Minnie Bruce Pratt

The distance between our work and our lives is often an invisible
border — one we cannot see or simply refuse to see. Our creativity is
what encourages us to seek shelter and understanding in new worlds.
Too often we cannot return to the old land, language, or even memory.
To be a poet is to love, to pursue desire, to soar above the landscape
and territory of flags and anthems. There is a hunger in the heart of
almost every man and woman. How many hands must we push away
from our mouths as we enter the 21st century?

....E. Ethelbert Miller

Rolling Pennies

They're survivors; the room is rich
with their praise – a cloud of copper,
fragrant as boxwoods or incense.
They slide, 2-4-6-8-10, 2-4-6-8-20,
into a roll. The count grows into a chant
that takes my hands. This might be knitting,
but there won't be any thing in the end.
94's ching against those that wear
green tarnish like a beard.

Whose lint have they gathered?
Some, figuring in nickel bets, were passed
at playgrounds: "You can too see Lincoln
in the memorial." Or held in open palms,
spared from sacrifice on train tracks,
maybe in Eisenhower's second term.

At a 1960 I see a child catching
a glint of mica at the side of a road.
He held it to the light, barely breathing,
to read messages from the mineral world.
I slide that old penny into the roll,
a miner in reverse, and count.

....*Sunil Freeman*

Flying the Zuni Mountains
[excerpt]

This we know:
we are the wind.
We will come back gently over the lake,
we will lash the waves and bend the trees;
we will lie side by side on the high mountains
drinking martinis and telling the old jokes over.
Never our wings will melt or crumple with heat or hardness.
This we know.
For the man who draws the blueprints, shapes the wings,
    threads the bolts, pulls the props
is not our faith.
Ours is the wind and the wind is us
and no one shall bury us ever.

We have known space not surrounded by closets and
cabbages cooking,
we have whirled rainbows over our heads;
we have owned the earth by rising from it,
never again shall we walk with ordinary feet.

The wings were shaped from a woman's weeping...
no other tears shall fall.

.....Ann Darr

Why I Never Take Off My Watch at Night

(1)

Our dog, left home alone too long,
would worry all the things that held
the scent of my son – pajamas, a blanket,
socks, and once a baseball bat –
into a pile inside the front door.
He'd sleep on that pile in the dark
and wait for the right high pitch
of pistons ticking up our street.

(2)

Keep in touch, we tell the young men as we send them
off to our wars. Then the remote-controlled TV
tells us what they touch in their pockets:
a braid of hair, a plastic cross, the picture
of a girl, a tiny Bible, a smooth stone
from the crawl-space underneath the house.

(3)

I like to grope a little, scare myself
by crossing over borders without maps until
I do not know the language of the place.
I wear the smell of being lost
in ancient streets, connected to nothing
except a distant drum-tap
from the far red outpost of the wrist,
the thready little rhythm to go home to.

(4)

Sometimes when I sail, grey silk begins to move
between the little boat and everywhere,
and I'm too far out to hear the strum of breakers,
so I try to get the sense of something regular
and fix upon the beating light that's shoreward,
sure that I've left it not too far away.

.....Rod Jellema

You Are

My anchor my magnetic north
My coming home my setting forth
To my old craft the turning star
You are middle distance near and far
Lullaby sleep and reveille
My waking laughter ecstasy
My coming home and setting forth
My anchor and magnetic north

.....Roland Flint

DNA

Like beads
strung out in
patient replication
adenine guanine
cytosine   thymine
guanine   cytosine
adenine   thymine
cytosine....
4 character alpha
bet for mystic
WORD
evoking
hair eyes nails
lungs intestines dreams
the myriad shapes of
cells
the forms of men
and with those men
of gods, of worlds beyond
of means of speech
and codes beyond the code
beyond the
CODE

....Frank Evans

Baby Leopard

Every day I eat the zookeeper's food
Away from the grasslands of my rightful home,
Separated even from the zebra.

Every day the overwhelming tide of people
Swarm in from the gates.
They look at me and pass without a word.
Nobody cares what I think
under my green plastic canopy.

.....*Adam Chambers*

Arithmetic

Once numbers were fun –
5 was orotund,
always holding forth to 6
who'd slide downhill,
rolling head over heels into 7
who'd stand ramrod straight,
not like that snaky 8,
even slipperier than 6
who'd do a backflip and turn
into 9 with its bulging top,
a tipsy lollipop, a ring
escaping its finger.

Now we're into subtraction,
that reckoning of loss.
I see a child who lets go
of a balloon and watches it fly
out of reach, past trees
and into the sky. His mouth

opens in a perfect O of disbelief,
and out come all the vowels of grief.

.....Nan Fry

blessing the boats

at St. Mary's

may the tide
that is entering even now
the lip of our understanding
carry you out
beyond the face of fear
may you kiss
the wind then turn from it
certain that it will
love your back   may you
open your eyes to water
water waving forever
and may you in your innocence
sail through this to that

.....Lucille Clifton

Broken Wing

It was in front of the house where I grew up,
at the base of the big tree, a brown baby bird.
Not even 8 year old curiosity could find its mother.
So carefully, I stepped toward it,
watched its small, unmoving feathers,
its dark, unblinking eyes. After a few silent minutes
I scooped it up
gently. It was all heart
pounding against the cup of my palm.
Years later my parents abandoned the house,
married other people. The tree still stands
and I remember the moment, the bird's heart
pounding in my palm, its dark eyes
constant, looking for what is lost.

.....Virginia Crawford

A Poem For My Father

It could only have been you
Who lifted me to the high, thick branches
Strong enough to hold my weight

The cherry tree all in bloom,
A white ship on a green sea
Tacking north

And there among the murmur of bees' wings
I climbed through a cloud of blossom and

into the white heart of spring

....Michael Fallon

Shapes, Vanishings

1

Down a street in the town where I went
to high school twenty-odd years ago, by doorways
and shadows that change with the times, I walked
past a woman at whose glance I almost stopped cold,
almost to speak, to remind her of who I had been—
but walked on, not being certain it was she,
not knowing what I might find to say.
It wasn't quite the face I remembered, the years
being what they are, and I could have been wrong.

2

But that feeling of being stopped cold, stopped dead,
will not leave me, and I hark back
to the thing I remember her for, though God knows
how I could remind her of it now.
Well, one afternoon when I was fifteen
I sat in her class. She leaned on her desk,
facing us, the blackboard behind her arrayed
with geometrical figures – triangle, square,
pentagon, hexagon, et cetera. She pointed
and named them. "The five-sided figure," she said,
"is a polygon." So far so good, but then when she said,
"The six-sided one is a hexagon," I wanted things clear.
Three or more sides is *poly*, I knew, but five only
is *penta*, and said so; she denied it,
and I pressed the issue, I, with no grades
to speak of, a miserable average to stand on
with an Archimedean pole – no world to move,
either, just a fact to get straight, but she
would have none of it, saying at last, "Are you
contradicting me?"

3

A small thing to remember a teacher for. Since then,
I have thought about justice often enough
to have earned my uncertainty about what it is,
but one hard fact from that day has stayed with me:
If you're going to be a smartass, you have to be right,
and not just some of the time. "Are you
contradicting me?" she had said, and I stopped
breathing a moment, the burden of her words
pressing down through me hard and quick, the huge
weight of knowing I was right, and beaten. She
had me. "No, ma'am," I managed to say, wishing
I had the whole thing down on tape to play back
to the principal, wishing I were ten feet tall
and never mistaken, ever, about anything in this world,
wishing I were older, and long gone from there.

4

Now I am older, and long gone from there.
What sense is a grudge over something so small?
What use to forgive her for something
she wouldn't remember? Now students
face me as I stand at my desk, and the shoe
may yet find its way to the other foot,
if it hasn't already. I couldn't charge
thirty-five cents for all that I know
of geometry; what little I learned is gone now,
like a face looming up for a second out of years
that dissolve in the mind like a single summer.
Therefore,
if ever she almost stops me again,
I will walk on as I have done once already,
remembering how we failed each other,
knowing better than to blame anyone.

....Henry Taylor

Prizes

My children chase seagulls along the sand,
pigeons the length of the park. They sneak up
behind the birds, their eyes gleaming,
their faces bold as spring.

I wonder what I would do if they caught
one of those things, their small fingers
enfolding the soft belly of the bird
as they carried it to me like a prize

saying, "Daddy, look what we've done.
Daddy, can we bring it home?"
What choice would there be? That thing
is dirty, perhaps diseased; the beak sharp,

and the bird did not want to be caught.
But the birds flutter out of reach before
the children even feel feathers. My smile
becomes so fatherly it frightens me.

I buy some peanuts from the vendor in the park,
tear the bag open with my teeth, divide
them among my children. "Here," I say,
"I loved these when I was a kid."

They look at me, puzzled,
take the peanuts and when they think
I'm not watching, toss them to the pigeons,
their eyes gleaming, their faces bold as spring.

....Michael S. Glaser

I Took My Cousin to Prettyboy Dam

I took my cousin to Prettyboy Dam.
A boxer was swimming for sticks, the ripples
Blew from the left, and beer cans glittered
Under the poison-ivy.

We talked of pelota; and how the tendrils of vines
Curl opposite ways in the opposite hemispheres.
My cousin was dying.   By this I mean
The rate of his disengagement was rapid.

There was a haze of heat, and August boys
Chunked rocks at a bottle that bobbed on the water.
The slow hours enclosed the flight of instants,
Melted the picnic-ice.

Everything he saw differently, and more clearly than I.
The joined dragonflies, the solid foam of the fall;
The thin haste of the ant at my foot,
And me, as I looked at him.

We were close beside each other, speaking of
Pelota, chaining cigarettes when the matches were gone.
But we saw different things, since one could not say
"Wait...."
Nor the other "Come...."

...Josephine Jacobsen

On Assateague Island

we sipped
the late night
skinny
down
along
the open
coast
and wet
laid back
the stars
unzipped
the old
green tent
and then
there were
wild horses

....Charles Rossiter

Horse Girls

1.

The only year I want a pony for Christmas,
my mother is crying, she asks me
for permission to leave.

I picture her for a moment, lifted up to sit behind a cowboy,
astride and waving, laughing even,
but I do not let her go.

She saddles me daily, in silence and rides me to school,
with her own careful stitching in the tackle.
The bridle reminds me to be pleasant.
She bits herself up to smile at the ladies in the
grocery store, though she talks to none of them.

and she stays and stays and stays

2.

Near the Grand Canyon, my forehead on the glass of the car window,
my chin on the blue vinyl of my parents' car, riding west.
I see you. All of you moves:
your tail is actually whipping, your mane is honestly shaking
and you are genuinely the black of agate.
You are the only wild thing I have ever seen.
I watch for as long as I can see you.

3.

When I played at her house,
she owned plastic horses,
our hands rode them
over the fields of clean wall to wall
while her mother vacuumed.

Inside my room,
I wished for carpeting
and long hair like hers.
I didn't wish for long though.

I could see, even then,
the fence posts my mother was digging holes for,
the turn of her pliers barbing the wire,

the thing she was grooming me to be.

.....Maggie Polizos

Fledgling

Mother-may-I is not a game my son can play this fall.
Without permission, he strides toward endings, takes giant steps.
Can he be this slender man turning to me the clear eyes of my child?
The car crests the last, long ridge of hills and we sweep
down into the mountain valley he will soon think of as home.
He does not see a woman, stricken as Demeter, who knows how barren earth

will be this winter. He only looks to share his joy in country earth,
pungent with wood smoke and cider apples, smoldering with fall.
We jolt a rutted lane where honeysuckle thickets are the home
of startled quail. A peevish groundhog waddles down the steps
a sagging porch dips gingerly in the deep grass, as we sweep
up to a sun blistered frame house. "Needs some paint," says my child.

He waits my wan smile, then enter 'man of action' exit 'child',
lopes to a tire sprouting frost black tomatoes, pokes the earth
to find the key. I am ushered in with a deep bow, the sweep
of plumes. He glowers as he watches my face fall
at the blotches of mildew on the walls, cobweb festooned steps,
a sofa belching stuffing where field mice found a home.

Above the mantle, wreathed in flowers, 'Home Sweet Home',
cardboard stained behind splintered glass. It shall be for my child
I vow, grab mop and bucket to hurry up the steps.
I wipe the grime from windows, dreaming how soft this valley earth
will grow with apple bloom next spring. House cleaning spring and fall –
my mother battled soot and tarnish. "And we'll sweep

the cobwebs out of the sky," I hear her croon while I sweep
dried raisin flies from the larder in the home
of a goodwife spider. The toothpick bones of mice fall
onto my dust pan from a closet shelf. I wonder, will my child
remember, when I, too, am gone from earth,
his mother, kerchief askew, resting on these steps?

My son carries an armload of fire wood up the steps.
I rise to stand beside him, lift a hand to sweep
his cowlick flat, laugh at his astonished, "How on earth – "
He stares at scrubbed pine floors, the sunlit windows of his home,
then crunches me in the convulsive hug of a child.
I relish his transparent happiness. I will not let one tear fall.

We sit, shoulders touching, on the steps of his new home.
To the star sweep I say a silent, "*Vale Valeque*, child
of earth," for a moment grasp a God who lets sparrows fall.

....Marta Knobloch

I Don't Want to Grow Up

I don't want to grow up
because grownups have to do
too much work. Every day
they have to go to work, clean the house,
fix the food, and change the baby's pampers
when he stinks!

I'd rather be a kid
because when you're a kid you get lots of toys
and get to go outside and climb trees,
and ride a bike, and you don't have to go get food
and you don't have to call people names
or check the mail for bills.

....*Dewitt Clinton*

What I Am Waiting For

To linger longest; to be
still and quiet and good enough,
so that, one by one, the lights will flicker
and go out, at last, in that house: doors
rusted and slipped from their hinges, the old porch
giving way to rain, old angers falling away to silence;

I'll approach it then, the rough-
hewn house of my childhood, emptied,
dark, shutters banging in the wind;
I'll place my hand on the bannister,
and slowly climb, unpunished,
up the groaning stairs to a room that was mine;

I'll lie down on the bed and watch
the stars come out again
through that one small window
where the safe world once glistened
and shone beyond me like the God I prayed to
who did not save me from anything;

Maybe then the knots in me
will come undone; maybe I will
be so whole for once I'll sleep all night
though the owls screech in the moony trees
and the weasels call out to each other again and again
far off in the complicated dark.

....Anne Caston

Evening Marshes

Marsh grass is golden
Under a late sun,
And wild ducks' wings
Whistle with the wind.
We are one,
Wild duck and setting sun,
Marsh grass around the pond,
Earth smells and shadows,
Coming cold and early night,
Evening star and this
Great emptiness
Within me.

....Gilbert Byron

As a writer, skin has defined what I do because as soon as I open my front door and go out into the world, I'm no longer a private animal who would love to just delight in nature and notions about God and sanity. When I go out the front door, I'm received in a particular way -- as a black male -- and I must face the world and history; I must listen, and my voice must negotiate with that wider world.

....*Fred D'Aguiar*

Embracing the millennium surely means moving into it with love. It means moving into it with confidence and hope, with some kind of vision of what we want to become as a people on this bright blue planet.

....*Sara Ebenreck*

Poem for My Sons

When you were born, all the poets I knew
were men, dads eloquent on their sleeping
babes and the future: Coleridge at midnight,
Yeats' prayer that his daughter lack opinions,
his son be high and mighty, think and act.
You've read the new father's loud eloquence,
fiery sparks written in a silent house
breathing with the mother's exhausted sleep.

When you were born, my first, what I thought was
milk: my breasts sore, engorged, but not enough
when you woke. With you, my youngest, I did not
think: my head unraised for three days, mind-dead
from waist-down anesthetic labor, saddle
block, no walking either.
                              Your father was then
the poet I'd ceased to be when I got married.
It's taken me years to write this to you.

I had to make a future, willful, voluble,
lascivious, a thinker, a long walker,
unstruck transgressor, furious, shouting,
voluptuous, a lover, a smeller of blood,
milk, a woman mean as she can be some nights,
existence I could pray to, capable of
poetry.
          Now here we are. You are men,
and I am not the woman who rocked you
in the sweet reek of penicillin, sour milk,
the girl who could not imagine herself
or a future more than a warm walled room,
had no words but the pap of the expected,
and so, those nights, could not wish for you.

But now I have spoken, my self, I can ask
for you: that you'll know evil when you smell it;
that you'll know good and do it, and see how both
run loose through your lives; that then you'll remember
you come from dirt and history; that you'll choose
memory, not anesthesia; that you'll have work
you love, hindering no one, a path crossing
at boundary markers where you question power;
that your loves will match you thought for thought
in the long heat of blood and fact of bone.

Words not so romantic nor so grandly tossed
as if I'd summoned the universe to be
at your disposal.
                          I can only pray:

That you'll never ask for the weather, earth,
angels, women, or other lives to obey you;

that you'll remember me, who crossed, recrossed
you,
            as a woman making slowly toward
an unknown place where you could be with me,
like a woman on foot, in a long stepping out.

                          ....Minnie Bruce Pratt

Tears

"Save us from tears that bring no healing..."
Matthew Arnold

When the ophthalmologist told me gravely
that I didn't produce enough tears,
I wanted to say: but I cry too much
and too often. At airports and weddings
and sunsets. At bad movies

where the swell of sentimental music
forces open my tear ducts
like so many locks in a canal.
And when he handed me this vial
of artificial tears, I wanted to tell him

about Niobe. Perhaps if her tear ducts
had been deficient, she wouldn't
have dissolved into salty water
after the loss of her children.
Maybe other heroes and heroines

deprived of the resonant ability to cry
would have picked themselves up
and acted sensibly. Othello for instance
weeping, before he killed her,
into Desdomona's embroidered pillow.

And so I take this bottle of distilled grief
and put it in the back of a drawer,
but I don't throw it away. There may be poems
in my future that need to be watered,
for I still remember Tennyson

who wrote of how short swallow-flights of song
dip their wings in tears, and skim away.

.....Linda Pastan

118

Mommy's Bracelet

Michael Millner,
I dedicate this poem
to you.
Michael Millner,
we have not
forgotten you.

Mommy's bracelet;
stainless steel wrapped
around her left wrist,
just below her watch.
There is a space where
the two ends meet, curved
metal just barely touching.

I am six: I trace
the letters engraved
on the metal, pretend
it is Braille, too young
to read with eyes open.
"What does it say Mommy?
Is it from Daddy?
Is it about me?"

Mommy pulls her hand
away and looks at her
wrist, as if checking
the time.
"It says S/FC Michael Millner.
11/29/67.
It's not from Daddy.
It's not about you."

"But who is Michael...?"

She does not answer, looking
at something far away, or not
looking at all.
She is quiet.

I grow quiet.

I am thirteen: in school,
we are learning about
the Vietnam War. 1967...
I ask again about her bracelet.

"It's a POW/MIA bracelet.
Thousands were given out
during and after the war –
police action. We're not
to take them off until
something is found –
dogtags, papers...remains –
and they are no longer
lost." She holds the
bracelet, wrapping the fingers
of her right hand around
it, around her wrist.

"Is there a bracelet for everyone
who was lost? How do you know
if they were found? What
if they don't want to be
found? Will I inherit
the bracelet?"

She sets her book down
in front of her. "Sometimes,
if they find...someone,
it's in the newspaper. I check.
I'm sure he would want to be
found; he has a wife and
two children. I don't
know if you will inherit
it – let's hope they find him."
She looks at her wrist again,
briefly, then picks up the book.

I am twenty-two and I
am writing a poem about
my mother's bracelet.
I call her, asking for
the date on it; the name
I still remember.
She reads it to me
over the phone, then asks
"Do you want to know
the rest?"

Michael Millner had just
signed up for another
tour when he was reported
missing.
Michael Millner's two children,
four and six when he was lost,
both needed counseling,
both needed to hear that Daddy may
never come home, but not
because he didn't love
them, or because they had done
something wrong.

Michael Millner's wife
years after his disappearance
was engaged; she spent
seven years looking at herself
each night in the mirror,
not knowing if she was
a widow
or an adulteress; she
broke the engagement.

When the Wall in Washington
was dedicated, Michael Millner's
son marched in the honor guard,
proudly wearing the uniform
his father once wore, may still wear,
may be buried in.

"Do they still find people Mom?
Do you ever take the bracelet off?"

"Sometimes in the paper
it will say they found
a mass grave in a barn
somewhere, or a soldier
who'd gone native, married
a local girl, disappeared.

"No, I don't take it off."

Michael Millner, my mother
wears your name
just over her steady pulse.
Each time she looks at her watch
to check the time
she sees decades
thirty-two years of
stainless steel
trying to seal the gaps in
her generation in
her faith in
the world.

Michael Millner
we have not
forgotten you.
Michael Millner
I dedicate this poem
to you.

.....*Lauri Watkins*

The Wave

Memorial Stadium, Baltimore, 1991

Vendors with racks of soft drinks, palettes
of cotton candy, ice cream in bright insulated
bags, pretzels in metal cabinets, and the peanut
man with his yellow peanut earring. Money folded

between fingers, spokes of green waving
in the glad pandemonium greeting the Budman
with his quick-pouring mechanism strapped
to his wrist like a prosthesis, or the hot-dog guy

genuflecting in the steep aisles, anointing
the roll and weenie with mustard before passing
it down to the skinny kid sitting between fat parents.
In the air above us the flittering birds attracted

and repelled by planetary field lights, swoop
in ecstatic arcs, trapped under a dark invisible dome.
The park organ, the Jumbo-tron, the mascot
pacing atop the visitors' dugout, taunting them

with over-sized antics, while the groundskeepers
spray the infield with a fire hose, leavening
the calm, raked earth... Later, in the fifth
or sixth, two soldiers sitting next to me, who

have paced each other with a beer-an-inning and kept
their buzz buffed with a flask, take off their shirts,
though the night's cool, and move to the front row,
where they turn, face the crowd, and sweep up

their arms, commanding us to rise from our seats.
At first only a few respond, but like molecules quickening
or cells dividing or a herd stampeding, we coalesce –
orison provoking unison – section by section, as if

township by township, our standing up and sitting down,
becomes the Simon Says and Mother-May-I? of a nation,
as it runs through our rippling, shimmering, upraised hands
that form the crest of a wave built on the urges

and urgings of the soldiers whose skin is slick
with sweat or some other laborious issue and whose goal
now, for all of us, for themselves, for the players on the field,
is simply to stay in the wave, to keep it going for as long as they can.

....Michael Collier

What Grandma Said

Once Grandma told me she was afraid of dying,
a great secret since church was her avocation.
At the time she was standing
in the scarred doorway, lintels
much-painted to cover the stabs
of sabre and knives
from the Civil War,
between her kitchen
with its black iron stove,
and the dining room
where she often sat by the radio
in a rocking chair, tatting, the tiny shuttle
flying magically as she made lace.

By then, the Civil War was far back in time,
and the fact soldiers had been billeted
in this oldest part of the house,
that it had been used as a hospital,
this familiar space part of a battleground,
astonished me,
the smell of blood and fear
long replaced with the aroma of roasts
and pies from the range.

When I was older, I imagined Walt Whitman,
a nurse in the War, in this room,
his beautiful piercing eyes,
the beard hiding his poems,
that old lilac at Grandma's back door,
the one of which he wrote – who knows,
the fantasy was sweet.

But that Grandma was afraid of dying,
of Heaven, the aftermath of her life,
after all those Sundays at church on her knees
frightened me, as it touched me,
for by then she had lost so many,
too many to count,
But Grandma was human.
Thank God she could not foresee
the future that day, as she rallied her faith,
proclaiming her desire to die with her boots on,
(her phrase, military, fitting,
in that old battle-room), couldn't know
that she was doomed to die
two deaths instead of one,
fated to lie in the twilight of coma
for seven years before the blessed respite
of death finally came.

....*Irene Rouse*

The Song of the Word

To my ancestors of the Southern Riverlands of the Chesapeake....
who addressed the right enemy for all the wrong reasons.

At the Battle of Antietam....

They went up to the mountains and crossed Potomac wide.
Captive of the dreams this nation would divide.
In defiance of creation, allied in the absurd,
each song would seek its ending as their flesh became the word.

Kin and kind....
left their dreams and loves behind.
On a dusty road to glory, in close-ordered ranks conspired
to descend in contradictions, falling ever....reaching higher.
Consumed by word, by water, and by fire!

And to their sons and daughters in all these waters
in this foreground of staging, facing the millennial
battle to sustain and maintain the Chesapeake Creation

May you go up to the mountain, and cross the waters wide.
Become the captain of your dreams and all the songs you hold inside.
May your dream be of creation and of the voice you've heard,
saying: "you are the beginning and the beginning is the word!"

Word will turn!
Turning will conspire!
To reach into the darkness awakening desire,
and arise from contradiction, reaching high, and then go higher.
You are the word, the water, you're the fire!!!

....Tom Wisner

Acknowledgements

Karren LaLonde Alenier's poem, "Looking for Divine Transportation," first appeared in her book, <u>Looking for Divine Transportation</u> (The Bunny and Crocodile Press, 1991), then in <u>Bumper Cars: Gertude Said She Took Him For a Ride</u> (Mica Press). It is reprinted here with permission of the author.

Renée Ashley's poem, "Charity," first appeared in *Poetry*. The poem is reprinted with permission of the author.

Ned Balbo's poem, "First Days in a World," appears in his book, <u>Galileo's Banquet</u> (Washington Writers' Publishing House, 1998). The poem is reprinted with permission of the author.

Alan Britt's poem, "Rural Maryland," first appeared in *Folio* and is reprinted here with permission of the poet.

Sterling Brown's poem, "After Winter," appears in <u>The Collected Poems of Sterling A. Brown</u> (Tri-Quarterly Press, 1989) and is reprinted with permission of the poet, to HoCoPoLitSo (1982).

Gilbert Byron's poem, "Evening Marshes," first appeared in <u>These Chesapeake Men</u> (The Driftwood Press, North Montpelier, Vt., 1943). It is reprinted here with permission of Chesapeake College where his papers are housed.

Kenneth Carroll's poem, "Montana Terrace," first appeared in his book, <u>So What</u> (The Bunny and the Crocodile Press, 1997), © retained by the author, reprinted with permission of the author.

Grace Cavalieri's "Don't Undersell Yourself" was first published in <u>Why I Cannot Take a Lover</u> (The Washington Writers' Publishing House, 1975), and "This Is" was first published in <u>Creature Comforts</u> (The Word Works, Inc., 1982). Both poems are copyrighted by and reprinted with permission of the author.

Maxine Clair's poem, "Harriet Tubman Said," first appeared in <u>Coping with Gravity</u> (Washington Writer's Publishing House, 1988), © Maxine Clair, reprinted with permission of the author.

Lucille Clifton's poems "blessing the boats" and "we are running" both appear in quilting (Boa Editions, Ltd., 1991), © retained by the author, reprinted with permission of the author.

Michael Collier's poem, "The Wave," first appeared in his book, The Ledge (Houghton Mifflin), and is reprinted here with permission of the publisher and the author.

Geraldine Connolly's poem, "Lydia," first appeared in *Poetry* and was later published in her book, Food for the Winter (Purdue University Press, 1990), © retained by the author, reprinted with permission of the author.

Bruce Curley's poem, "The Kind of Woman to Marry," first appeared in Messages From the Heart. It is reprinted here with permission of the author.

Ann Darr's poem, "Flying the Zuni Mountains," is excerpted from "Flying the Zuni Mountains" which appears in her book, Flying the Zuni Mountains (Forest Woods Media Productions, 1994), © Anne Darr, reprinted with permission of the author.

Toi Derricotte's poem, "Christmas Eve: My Mother Dressing," appears in her book, Captivity (University of Pittsburgh Press, 1989), and is reprinted here with permission of the author.

Michael Fallon's poem, "A Poem for My Father," first appeared in his book, A History of the Color Black (Dolphin Moon Press, 1991), © retained by the author, reprinted with permission of the author.

Sunil Freeman's poem, "Rolling Pennies," first appeared in his chapbook, Surreal Freedom Blues (Argonne Hotel Press, R.D. Baker Publisher, 1999), © Sunil Freeman, reprinted with permission of the author.

Eva Glaser's poem, "Waking," was first published in *The Christian Science Monitor* and is reprinted here with permission of the author.

Barbara Goldberg's poem, "The Miracle of Bubbles," was first published in her book, Cautionary Tales (Dryad Press, 1990), © retained by the author, reprinted with permission of the author.

Josephine Jacobsen's poem, "Prettyboy Dam," appeared in her book, The Animal Inside (Ohio University Press, 1966) and then in The Sisters: new and selected poems (The Bench Press, 1987). It is reprinted here with permission of the author.

Marijane Ricketts' poem, "Taken From the Top," is an excerpt from "Mountain Climbing in a Buick," which was first published in *Pegasus Review*, and is reprinted with permission of the author.

Charles Rossiter's poem, "On Assateague Island," was first published in *Atelier* and is reprinted here with permission of the author.

Sam Schmidt's poem, "Poetry Sends Her Love," first appeared in *Black Moon*, and is reprinted with permission of the author.

Myra Sklarew's poem, "Poem of the Mother," was first published in her book, Lithuania: New & Selected Poems (1997). It is reprinted with permission of the author.

Elizabeth Spires' poem, "Thanksgiving Night: St. Michael's," was first published in her book Annonciade (Viking Penguin, 1989), and is reprinted here with permission of the author.

Henry Taylor's poem, "Shapes, Vanishings," © 1986 by Henry Taylor, is reprinted from The Flying Change by permission of the author and Louisiana State University Press.

Hilary Tham's poem, "The Thrower of Stones" was first published in the e-zine: *poetrymagazine.com*. It appears here with permission of the author.

Kathy Wagner's poem, "Returning to the City By Boat," was first published in *Southern Poetry Review*. It is reprinted here with permission of the author.

Michael Waters', "The Mystery of Caves," first appeared in *Poetry* and then in Anniversary of the Air (Carnegie Mellon University Press, 1985). It is reprinted with permission of the author.

Julia Wendell's poem, "Fires at Yellowstone," first appeared in *Hayden's Ferry Review* and then in her book Wheeler Lane (Igneus Press, 1998), and is reprinted with permission of the author.

Reed Whittemore's "Still Life" appeared most recently in The Past, The Future, The Present (University of Arkansas Press), © 1990 by Reed Whittemore. It is reprinted with permission of the author.

Tom Wisner's lyric "Song of the Word" is published with permission of Tom Wisner, Chesapeake Studios. Music is available from Tom Wisner Studios, Box 7, California, MD 20619; chestory@earthlink.net.

Karen LaLonde Alenier is author of four collections of poetry including her latest, <u>Looking for Divine Transportation</u>. Lincoln College awarded her the first Billie Murray Denny Award for poetry. She is president of The Word Works.

Tyler Anderson was in fourth grade at Park Hall Elementary School in St. Mary's County when he wrote "Lies."

Renée Ashley's book, <u>SALT</u>, won the Brittingham Prize in Poetry, and her second collection, <u>The Various Reasons of Light</u>, was chosen as the inaugural poetry book for Avocet, Inc. She received a 1997-98 fellowship from the National Endowment of the Arts and her work is included in the Pushcart Prize XXIV.

Ned Balbo holds degrees from Vassar College, the Writing Seminars at Johns Hopkins, and the University of Iowa Writers' Workshop. He teaches at Loyola College in Baltimore and works as an academic dean for the Johns Hopkins Center for Talented Youth. He is currently a literature panelist (arts organizations) for the Maryland State Arts Council

David Bergman is the author or editor of over a dozen books including three volumes of poetry, the latest of which is <u>Heroic Measures</u>. He teaches at Towson State University and lives in Baltimore City and Talbot County.

Alan Britt edits and publishes *Black Moon: Poetry of Imagination*. His book, <u>Bodies of Lightning</u>, was published in 1995. He serves as a Maryland State Arts Council Poet-in-the-Schools.

Sterling A. Brown was the first Afro-American Poet Laureate. His family owned a farm in Howard County where he spent many summers and holidays between 1911 and the 1940's. He taught at Howard University where he served as mentor for generations of black literary scholars and artists.

Gilbert Byron is often considered the Henry David Thoreau of the eastern shore of Maryland where he lived in a small cabin and observed the Chesapeake life around him. He wrote for over fifty years and died in 1991, three weeks short of his 88th birthday. His cabin/home is now being restored as a memorial to his life and work.

Kenneth Carroll is the D.C. site coordinator for WritersCorps, an arts and social service program founded by the NEA and AmeriCorps. He is past president of the African American Writers Guild. His book, <u>So What! for the white dude who said this ain't poetry</u>, was published in 1997.

Anne Caston graduated from St. Mary's College of Maryland and earned an MFA from Warren Wilson College. Her book, <u>Flying Out With the Wounded</u>, was published by New York University Press in 1997. She served as the Jenny McKean Moore writer in residence at George Washington University and now teaches at the University of Alaska.

Grace Cavalieri, for twenty years the producer and host of WPFW's "The Poet and the Poem," is the author of ten books of poetry. She has written for opera, stage and film. Her awards include a PEN Fiction Award and the Allen Ginsberg Poetry Award. She is presently a writer for West Virginia Pubic Radio, and produces "The Poet and the Poem from the Library of Congress."

Adam Chambers was a fourth grade student at Mutual Elementary School in Calvert County when he wrote "Baby Leopard."

Katherine Chandler teaches environmental literature at St. Mary's College, and composition courses that focus on nature and the environment. She also teaches eighteenth and nineteenth century British literature. She is co-author of three young adult novels.

Maxine Clair lives in Landover. She has degrees from the University of Kansas and The American University. She teaches at George Washington University and her books are <u>Rattlebone</u> and <u>Coping with Gravity</u>.

Lucille Clifton is Distinguished Professor of Humanities at St. Mary's College of Maryland and she holds the Hilda C. Landers Endowed Chair in the Liberal Arts. A former poet Laureate of Maryland, she serves on the board of Chancellors of the Academy of American Poets, and is a Fellow of the American Academy of Arts and Sciences. Her most recent book is <u>Blessing the Boats: New and Selected Poems, 1988-2000</u>.

Dewitt Clinton was in the fourth grade at Park Hall Elementary School when he wrote "I Don't Want To Grow Up."

Jeffrey Lamar Coleman is on the English faculty at St. Mary's College of Maryland, and lives in Huntingtown, with his wife, Ynez. He holds an MFA in Creative Writing from Arizona State University and a Ph.D. in American Studies from the University of New Mexico.

Michael Collier is on the English faculty at the University of Maryland, and directs the Bread Loaf Writer's Conference. He is the author of four books of poetry, most recently The Ledge, published by Houghton Mifflin. He has received a Guggenheim fellowship and a Pushcart Prize, among other awards.

Geraldine Connolly resides in Montgomery County and teaches at the Writers Center and in the Maryland Poet-in-the-Schools program. She serves as executive editor of Poet Lore. Her books include The Red Room, Food for the Winter, and Province of Fire.

Virginia Crawford has a B.F.A. from Emerson and a Master of Letters from the University of St. Andrews in Scotland. She serves as a Poet-in-the-Schools for the Maryland State Arts Council, is co-founder of WordHouse and co-editor of Poetry Baltimore: poems about a city.

Bruce Curley lives in Germantown, Maryland with his wife Robin and sons Joshua, 14 and Eamon, 3. He works as a senior technical writer for DataSource, Inc. and has published in numerous literary journals.

Fred D'Aguiar was raised in Guyana, and currently teaches in the MFA program at the University of Miami. He has written five books of poetry, a play, and three novels, the latest of which is Feeding the Ghosts. His novel, The Longest Memory, won the Whitbread First Novel Award in Great Britain. A memoir of his appeared in Harper's.

Ann Darr lives in Bethesda, was an Air Force pilot during World War II and now teaches at American University and the Writer's Center. She has received a Discovery Award and Bunting and NEA Fellowships, has edited several anthologies, including Hungry As We Are, and has published eight collections of poetry, most recently Flying the Zuni Mountains.

Donna Denizé holds degrees from Stonehill College and Howard University. She has received grants from the Bread Loaf School of English, the D.C. Humanities Council and The Folger Shakespeare Library. She teaches at St. Albans School and has published the book, The Lover's Voice.

Toi Derricotte lived in Maryland for seven years and taught in the Maryland Poets-in-the-Schools program. She received grants from the Maryland State Arts Council and is currently on leave from the University of Pittsburgh to hold the Delta Sigma Theata Distinguished Chair at Xavier University. She is a co-founder of Cave Canem.

Neal Dwyer studied poetry at the University of Nice, France, and George Mason University. He teaches English at Charles County Community College, where he also publishes the *Connections* literary journal. His poems have appeared in *Tar River Poetry* and *The Iowa Review*.

Sara Ebenreck teaches philosophy at St. Mary's College of Maryland. Her interests lie in environmental philosophy, including its relationship to issues of justice and multi-cultural perspectives, women's voices in philosophy, and the intersection of spirituality and philosophy. She was co-founder and editor of the journal, *Earth Ethics*.

Sister Maura Eichner has spent a lifetime in Maryland, where —until her retirement— she taught in the Department of English at the College of Notre Dame of Maryland. She has published five books of poetry.

Frank Evans has published poems in *The Annapolis Papers,* Poetry at the Angle, *The Baltimore Gay Paper, BOGG,* and *River Styx.* He did medical research in Bethesda, practiced psychiatry in Annapolis, was medical director of a drug dependency program in Baltimore, and most recently has been a sub-investigator at a custom research organization.

Michael Fallon has taught creative writing at UMBC for the last 15 years. The founding editor of the *Maryland Poetry Review,* his first book of poems, A History of the Color Black, was published by Dolphin-Moon Press. His second book is titled, House of Forgotten Names. He lives in Baltimore City with his wife, Ruth.

Roland Flint is currently Poet Laureate of Maryland. Recently retired from Georgetown University where he was honored for his excellence as a teacher, he has several honorary doctorates, and his books have won much national recognition, including the National Poetry Series Award for his collection of poems, Stubborn. His most recent book is Easy.

Elizabeth Follin-Jones' stories, essays, and poetry have appeared in various journals including *Poet Lore, Passager,* and *Maryland Poetry Review.* Her chapbook, One Flight from the Bottom, won the 1990 Artscape poetry Award. She also works in sculpture and has lived in Chevy Chase since 1957.

Sunil Freeman earned a degree in journalism from the University of Maryland. His has published <u>That Would Explain the Violinist</u>, and the chapbook <u>Surreal Freedom Blues</u>. He works at The Writer's Center in Bethesda, Maryland.

Nan Fry has published two books, <u>Relearning the Dark</u> and <u>Say What I Am Called</u>. She received an Individual Artist's Award from the Maryland State Arts Council and has served as a Maryland Poet-in-the-Schools. She also teaches at The Writer's Center.

Maria Mazziotti Gillan is the founder and director of the Poetry Center at Passaic County Community College, editor of the *Paterson Literary Review*, and co-editor of the anthologies, <u>Unsettling America</u>, <u>Identity Lessons</u> and <u>Growing Up Ethnic in America</u>. She has published seven collections of poetry, most recently, <u>Where I Come From: New and Selected Poems</u>.

Eva Glaser was in the fourth grade at Hollywood Elementary School in St. Mary's County when she wrote "Waking."

Michael S. Glaser has taught at St. Mary's College of Maryland for over 30 years. As director of the Annual Ebenezer Cooke Poetry Reading, the Literary Festival at St. Mary's, and the VOICES reading series, he has brought nearly 300 poets and writers to read at the college. In 1995 Glaser received the Columbia Merit Award from the Poetry Committee of the Greater Washington, D.C. area for his service to poetry.

Barbara Goldberg is the author of five books, most recently <u>Marvelous Pursuits</u>. She has received two NEA fellowships and two PEN Syndicated Fiction awards, has served as Poet-in-Residence for Howard County, executive editor for *Poet Lore*, and editor-in-chief for the Word Works. Currently, she is executive speechwriter for AARP.

David Hilton is a professor of English at Anne Arundel Community College. He has published in numerous literary journals and has written six books of poetry, including <u>Huladance</u> and <u>No Relation to the Hotel</u>.

Robin Holland received her M.F.A. in poetry from Vermont College. She lives in Edgewater, Maryland, and has published nationally in literary journals. She now teaches cross-genre workshops in creativity and writing in public and private high school programs for visual artists.

Barbara Hurd is a professor of English at Frostburg State University. She co-edits *Nightsun* and directs both the Western Maryland Writers' Workshop and the Mountain Lake Writers' Festival. The recipient of several awards, including the 1994 ARTSCAPE award for <u>Objects in This Mirror</u>, her essay, "The Country Below," appears in the 1999 issue of <u>Best American Essays</u>.

Reuben Jackson works as an archivist with the Smithsonian's Duke Ellington Collection. He writes music reviews for several papers and his poetry has been anthologized in <u>Every Shut Eye Ain't Asleep</u>, <u>Unsettling America</u> and <u>In Search of Color Everywhere</u>. His book, <u>Fingering the Keys</u>, won the 1992 Columbia Book Award.

Josephine Jacobsen was Poetry Consultant to the Library of Congress from 1971 to 1973. She has published ten books of poetry, two of criticism (with William R. Mueller) four collections of short fiction, and one collected essays, criticism, and lectures. Among her many awards is a fellowship from The Academy of American Poets for service to poetry. Ms. Jacobson has lived in Baltimore for nearly 80 of her 91 years.

Philip K. Jason teaches literature and creative writing at the United States Naval Academy. Among his fifteen books are three volumes of poetry, most recently <u>The Separation</u>. He also writes about modern and contemporary poetry, war literature, and Anais Nin. From 1979-1998, he was editor or co-editor of *Poet Lore*.

Rod Jellema is professor emeritus of English literature at the University of Maryland, where he was founding director of the Creative Writing Program. He has written three books of poems, the latest of which is <u>The Eighth Day: New and Selected Poems</u>, and has received an award for his translations of Frisian poetry.

Marta Knobloch is the author of three collections of poetry: <u>The Song of What Was Lost</u> (ARTSCAPE Award, 1988), <u>Sky Pond</u> (Columbia Book Award, 1993), and <u>The Room of Months \ La atanza dei mesi</u> (Primio Donna di Ferrara, 1995). Her work has been widely published in the United States and abroad.

Ann B. Knox has published two books of poetry, <u>Stonecrop</u>, and <u>Staying is Nowhere</u>, and a collection of short stories, <u>Late Summer Break</u>. She lives in a cabin on the first folds of the Appalachians and is a long-time editor of *Antietam Review*.

Danuta E. Kosk-Kosicka writes and translates poetry in English and Polish. By training she is a biochemist. Until June, 1997 she was an associate professor in the School of Medicine at Johns Hopkins University and the University of Maryland at Baltimore. Her chapbook, <u>Here and There</u>, was published in 1999.

Kathryn Lange spent a year with AmeriCorps teaching environmental education for Langley Middle School on Whidbey Island in Puget Sound. She was selected a 1999-2000 Lannan Fellow and served as associate editor of the Maryland Millennial Anthology.

Merrill Leffler has been writing about marine science and the Chesapeake Bay since the early '80's. He is a founding member of The Writer's Center in Bethesda and publisher of Dryad Press. His books are <u>Partly Pandemonium, Partly Love</u>, and <u>Take Hold</u>.

Elizabeth Lund received an MFA from Cornell University. She is an editor and poetry reviewer for *The Christian Science Monitor*. Her poems have been widely published, and she has been a finalist for the Brittingham Prize and the Four Way Books Intro Prize. She teaches a poetry workshop at the Framingham Women's Prison in Massachusetts.

Laura Lynds lives in Glen Burnie, Maryland, with her husband, Charles, and daughter Amelia. Teacher, writer and flea market entrepreneur, she is currently homeschooling her daughter and grappling with the "true meaning of housework."

Kathy Mangan teaches writing and literature at Western Maryland College. Her poems have appeared in *The Georgia Review, The Gettysburg Review, Shenandoah, The Southern Review*, and <u>Pushcart Prize XV</u>. A collection of her poems, <u>Above the Tree Line</u>, was published by Carnegie Mellon University Press in 1995.

Anne McCauley was born and raised in southern Maryland, went to college in Connecticut, did an occupational therapy internship in the San Francisco city jail, and returned home where she works as an occupational therapist at St. Mary's Hospital.

William Meredith's first book of poems, <u>Love Letter from an Impossible Land</u>, was chosen by Archibald MacLeish in 1944 for the Yale Series of Younger Poets. Since then he has published ten additional collections of poetry, served as Poetry Consultant to the Library of Congress, and won a Pulitzer Prize. His most recent book, <u>Effort at Speech, New and Selected Poems</u> (Northwestern University Press), won the National Book Award for Poetry.

E. Ethelbert Miller is the director of the African American Resource Center at Howard University. Founder of the Ascension Poetry Reading Series, author of six books, including <u>Fathering Words: The Making of an African American Writer</u>, and the editor of three anthologies, his many awards include the O.B. Hardison Jr. Poetry Prize.

Ben Moldover was a junior at Thomas Wooton High School in Montgomery County when he wrote "Depression."

Jean Nordhaus was born in Baltimore. Her books of poetry include <u>My Life in Hiding,</u> <u>A Bracelet of Lies</u>, and <u>A Purchase of Porcelain</u>, about Moses Mendelssohn, which won the 1998 Kinloch Rivers Chapbook Competition.

Linda Pastan's 10th book of poems, <u>Carnival Evening: New and Selected Poems: 1968-1998</u> was published by Norton and was a finalist for The National Book Award. From 1991-1994 she served as Poet Laureate of Maryland.

Lara Payne grew up in Maryland and attended St. Mary's College of Maryland. She worked as an archeologist and teacher in Southern Maryland and Montgomery county and is currently in the MFA program in creative writing at New York University.

Kathy Pearce-Lewis lives in Bethesda and is an enthusiastic birdwatcher. Her poems have appeared widely in anthologies and magazines.

Maggie Polizos graduated from St. Mary's College of Maryland in 1994. She taught elementary school for several years in Los Angeles and in Washington D.C. and is currently a graduate student of The Johns Hopkins Writing Seminars in Baltimore.

Jacklyn W. Potter's work appears in several Paper-Mache Press anthologies and in <u>Hungry as We Are: Washington Area Poets</u> (WWPH). For sixteen years, she has directed the Joaquin Miller Poetry Series in Rock Creek Park.

Minnie Bruce Pratt is a widely respected feminist who has received numerous prizes and awards, including a Fulbright Fellowship, a Woodrow Wilson fellowship, and a nomination for the Pulitzer Prize for her five books of poetry, prose, and essays. She teaches as a member of the Graduate Faculty at the Union Institute in New Jersey. Her most recent book is <u>Walking Back Up Depot Street</u>.

Lia Purpura, a graduate of Oberlin College and The Iowa Writer's Workshop, is the author of The Brighter the Veil. Her collection of essays, Increase, won the AWP Award in nonfiction, and a new collection of her poetry, Stone, Sky, Listing will be published by the Ohio State University Press. She lives in Baltimore and teaches at Loyola College.

dj renegade (Joel Dias-Porter) became a professional disk jockey after leaving the USAF. He has performed his work on the Today Show, as well as in the feature film 'Slam' which won the Grand Jury Prize at the Sundance Film Festival in 1998.

Marijane Ricketts is a Garret County Greenblood after 30 years of Kensington life and Montgomery County schools. She is a past president of the Writer's League of Washington.

Kate Richardson taught at Charles Community College for ten years until she became a copywriter. She is a past director of the St. Mary's College Women-In-Poetry Program, and has, since 1980, lived on a farm in Calvert County that her father purchased in 1957.

Charles Rossiter is an NEA fellowship recipient and a widely published poet. He was born in Baltimore and now lives in Oak Park, Illinois. His most recent collection of poetry is Evening Stones.

Irene Rouse sells old books on the Internet. Her chapbook Private Mythologies was published in the summer of 1999. She is a contributing editor of WordWrites! magazine and a member of WordWrites! Traveling Poetry Road Show. In 1998 she received her M.A. in English from Salisbury State University in Maryland.

Karen Sagstetter is editor in chief for the Freer and Sackler Galleries, Smithsonian Institution, and editor of Asian Art & Culture. Author of two chapbooks of poetry and two nonfiction books, she won first prize in the fall 1998 Glimmer Train Press short story contest and is the recipient of a grant from the Maryland State Arts Council.

Sam Schmidt is the co-founder of WordHouse, a monthly poetry calendar and literary review for the Baltimore area, and hosts its weekly poetry series at the Minas Gallery. He is a recipient of a Maryland State Arts Council Grant and works for Johns Hopkins University Press.

Aurelie Sheehan is the author of the short story collection Jack Kerouac Is Pregnant. Her poetry and prose have been published in many literary magazines, and she has been anthologized in The Pushcart Prize XXIII: Best of the Small Presses 1999. She is the poetry and lectures coordinator at the Folger Shakespeare Library in Washington, D.C.

Edgar Silex holds an M.F.A. from the University of Maryland. He is the author of <u>Through All The Displacements</u>, and a chapbook, <u>Even The Dead Have Memories</u>. He has received fellowships from the NEA and the Maryland State Arts Council, and was the director of the Baltimore Literary Center, teaching creative writing and Native American mythology.

Myra Sklarew was born and raised in Baltimore and learned to love reading at the Enoch Pratt Library. She teaches at The American University and has written poetry, fiction, essays, and science articles.

Tracy Slaughter was in the sixth grade at Fallston Middle School in Harford County, Maryland when she wrote "Minnow."

Rose Solari is a poet, playwright, and fiction writer. Her chapbook, <u>The Stolen World</u>, won the 1993 Artscape Prize, and her book, <u>Difficult Weather</u>, was selected for the 1995 Columbia Prize for Poetry. Her recognitions include a University Prize from the A.A.P., and grants from the D.C. Commission on the Arts and Humanities, and the M.S.A.C. Her most recent publication is <u>Selections: Myths & Elegies</u>.

Elizabeth Spires lives in Baltimore and is a professor of English at Goucher College where she holds a Chair for Distinguished Achievement. She is the author of four books of poems: <u>Globe</u>, <u>Swan's Island</u>, <u>Annonciade</u>, and <u>Worldling</u>, and three books for children, <u>The Mouse of Amherst</u>, <u>With One White Wing</u>, and <u>Riddle Road</u>.

Robert Strott was born in Bethesda and attended St. Mary's College of Maryland. He has been an annual participant in the Literary Festival there since 1990; he considers it a pilgrimage.

Henry Taylor received the Pulitzer Prize in 1986 for his third collection of poetry, <u>The Flying Change</u>. He is professor of literature and co-director of the MFA Program in Creative Writing at American University in Washington, D.C.

Hilary Tham is the author of five books of poetry and a memoir. She has taught creative writing in Montgomery County, was HoCoPoLitSo's Visiting Poet to Howard County, and has been featured several times on cable TV. She teaches for the Writer's Center and is poetry editor of the *Potomac Review*.

Stacy Tuthill is the author of three collections of poems: House of Change, Necessary Madness, and Pennyroyal. She is also the author of The Taste of Smoke: Stories About Africa, and was a PEN Syndicated Fiction Winner. She has edited several anthologies, and is founding editor and publisher of Scop Publications.

Kathy Wagner was born in Baltimore and currently serves as an assistant professor of English at Washington College where she teaches creative writing, 20th century American literarture, and serves as director of gender studies. She lives in Chestertown, Md.

Michael Waters teaches at Salisbury State University. Recent publication includes New and Selected Poems (BOA Editions), and inclusion in the 7th edition of Contemporary American Poetry.

Lauri Watkins came from New York to Maryland where she was nurtured by the rivers of St. Mary's County and earned a B.A. from St. Mary's College. She is currently residing in Seattle.

Julia Wendell lives and works on a horse farm in Upperco. Her most recent collection of poems, Wheeler Lane, appeared from Igneus Press in 1998.

Reed Whittemore is a former Poet Laureate of Maryland as well as a former Poetry Consultant for the Library of Congress. He is a professor emeritus at the University of Maryland where he taught from 1967-1984. His most recent book is The Past, The Future, The Present (University of Arkansas Press, 1990).

Tom Wisner creates and records music specifically about Chesapeake waters and culture. Chesapeake Born and We've Got to Come Full Circle, his two earlier recordings, are now housed in the Smithsonian Folkways collection. A new CD of his Chesapeake music will be out in Spring 2000 from chestory@earthlink.net.

Brian Wood was a sophomore at Leonardtown High School in St. Mary's County when he wrote "my diRtY SaVIoR."